Withdrawn
Earlville Free Library

IN PRAISE OF SEASONS

A JOAN KAHN BOOK

Books by Alan H. Olmstead

IN PRAISE OF SEASONS

THRESHOLD: THE FIRST DAYS OF RETIREMENT

Portions of this work originally appeared in the Manchester (Conn.) *Evening Herald*.
Grateful acknowledgment is made for permission to reprint material on pages 1-2, 7-8, 9-10, 13, 17-19, 22, 30-32, 33-34, 35-36, 40-41, 43, 59, 68-69, 75-76, 80-82, 84-85, which originally appeared in *The New Yorker*. Copyright © 1959, 1962, 1963, 1964, 1965, 1966, 1967, 1968, 1969, 1970, 1971, 1972 by The New Yorker Magazine, Inc.

IN PRAISE OF SEASONS. Copyright © 1977 by Alan H. Olmstead. All rights reserved. Printed in the United States of America. No part of this book may be used or reproduced in an manner whatsoever without written permission except in the case of brief quotations embodied in critical articles and reviews: For information address Harper & Row, Publishers, Inc., 10 East 53rd Street, New York, N.Y. 10022. Published simultaneously in Canada by Fitzhenry & Whiteside Limited, Toronto.

FIRST EDITION

Designed by Lydia Link

Library of Congress Cataloging in Publication Data

Olmstead, Alan H
  In praise of seasons.
  1. Seasons. 2. Natural history. I. Title.
QB631.057   500.9   76-23515
ISBN 0-06-013284-1

77 78 79 80 10 9 8 7 6 5 4 3 2 1

IN PRAISE OF SEASONS

Alan H. Olmstead

Illustrations by Hamilton Kahn

HARPER & ROW, PUBLISHERS

NEW YORK, HAGERSTOWN, SAN FRANCISCO, LONDON

To Readers

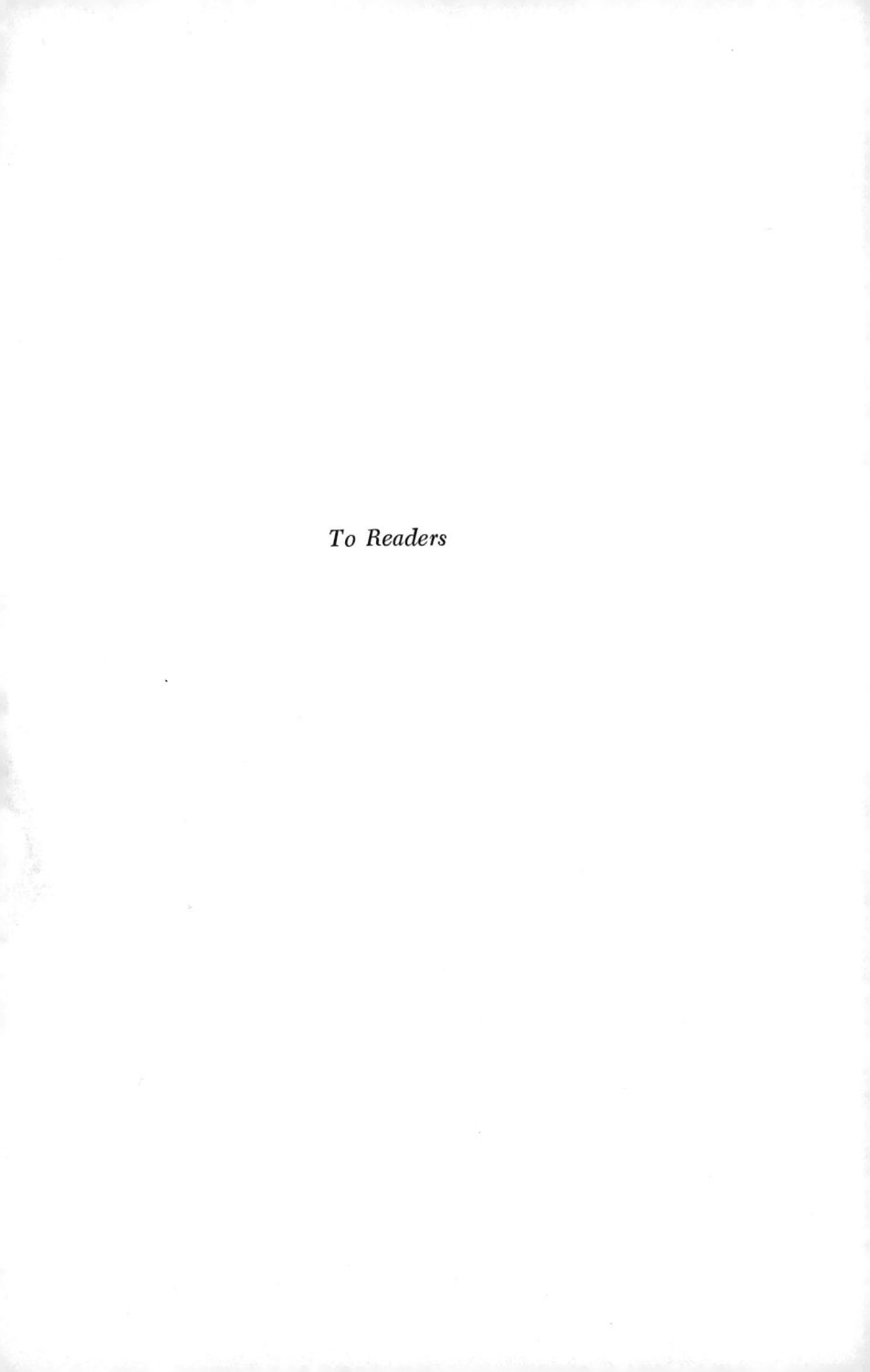

Preface

These reports of a relationship between one man and garden soil and hill and sky and bird and weather originally appeared as editorials in the Manchester (Conn.) *Evening Herald* or as "Connecticut Yankee" columns in that and other Connecticut newspapers, or as unsigned contributions to the "Notes and Comment" department of *The New Yorker*.

In a small circular pond, when the weather is completely windless and the surrounding trees, and even the birds in their branches, stand motionless, the water itself can be observed rotating, with a slight lag in comparison to the rotation that the earth beneath it is making. One sees the water move by watching what one thinks to be the movement of silt journeying clockwise past any point on the shore, or by studying the faintest of shimmers that appear where the dark reflections of overhanging tree branches lie on the surface of the pond.

There was also, in this bland twilight last evening, other movement, more pronounced and more reassuring to the senses than that of the slippage between earth and water. In a marsh half screened by last summer's sedge, a mallard and his mate had stepped out of the water and were preening themselves with slow archings of neck and stretchings of feathers. A dog ran the edges of the pond. The pond mirrored a high flight of blackbirds, who fled from one edge of the mirror to the other as if the dog had flushed them out of the bank on which he was working. The noise of peepers surged and ebbed back and forth across the water, in what seemed a physical movement. When one walked first to the inlet brook and then to the outlet dam, one could see that, in addition to the rotation of the body of water on its turntable earth, there was a ceaseless substitution of new water for old.

The final movement of the scene was that of a muskrat—Thoreau preferred the word "musquash"—ferrying produce from the outside swamp to some underwater delivery entrance. All this, we thought as we left—this rhythmic half-hour experience beside a pond—is as close to a definition of attainable peace as we are likely to get, whether it is at Walden in 1845, or in this century at a pond called Pearl.

And Green Quilt

Old friends sometimes drift into a tacit neglect of the normal courtesies, and, in the cold atmosphere of taking things for granted there occasionally comes a moment when such thoughtless expectation fails and friendship dies. Then, in retrospect, it may seem that working a little harder at the formal amenities might have protected the friendship.

It is in such a precautionary mood that, today, we take pains to greet the old friend who dropped in shortly after midnight. We want it understood that our handshake is firm, though moist. We are really glad to have such a guest. The arrival is pure joy; departure, if it has to come, will be a deprivation, and even the anticipatory thought of it is painful.

Our guest is welcome to the run of the whole house, and the pasture and the hill. The more this guest feels at home with us, the happier we shall be. As for the green quilt on the bed, and the canopy of stars, and the music by day and by night, and the garlands of flowers placed here and there, and the sweet scents, they are no effort at all, and for our own pleasure too. There must be, in this, more of life than in any other season. Welcome, summer.

Fireflies

Fireflies are big and bright this year, and this deviation from normalcy, coming into our summer nights without explanation, provides a modest but timely reinforcement to our will to believe in a world of the wonderful, in which anything can happen. If fireflies can suddenly equip themselves with such increased candlepower—we would say that as against the jelly glasses and Mason jars boys used to find adequate for firefly power it would take gallon jugs or carboys to do this year's Lampyridae justice—then other surprise increases in our natural resources are also possible. Last night we had company to dinner, but it would have been a waste of man-made kilowatts to turn the yard lights on. That meant so much less coal had to be mined, or oil pumped, or uranium fissioned, all thanks to a surprise firefly factor that suddenly offered cheaper, better illumination.

Bird-Watched

This is the time of year, as the corn plant begins to shape itself for yield, when we grow nervously conscious of sharp, knowing eyes relentlessly fixed on every move we make.

If, in a week or two, we go up to the cornfield carrying our usual assortment of old clothes, these eyes will note, shrewdly and amusedly, just what items we have marked for pointless sacrifice this year. They will observe, with professional judgment, the artistry with which we arrange these castoffs on a makeshift pole in the middle of the field. They will grow a little sardonic as they criticize our taste in hats, and as soon as we have finished and departed they will swoop in for closer examination and then get back to their usual business of stripping down the young ears of corn.

We are used to being under such scrutiny. We know when it is there, even if there is no telltale caw. We, and our most persistent bird watcher, are old friends. We always plant a few extra rows for him.

Some bird watchers, however, make us nervous. When the catbird takes his observation seat, we know we are in for an examination which has no other purpose than that of slightly malicious character analysis and we squirm, as if our spirit were naked.

And as the bittern, out in the pasture, keeps an eye on the progress of our chores, and we think of his redoubtable prowess with claw, we have the feeling of being threatened with actual attack.

Of all the bird watchers, we like the orioles best. They do their watching in fast streaking pairs, with many swift changes of perspective and angle, quite as if they considered us a handsome subject, and were only waiting for the perfect picture to put in their family elm.

The Good Soaking

Gardeners are hard to please, and one reason for that is that almost every blessing (of sun or rain) we seek can, given in excess, turn to a curse (of drought or flood).

We remember back to last winter and how we longed for the hot sun of June. That looked-for sun, in the past few weeks, has been dealing as much death as life, as much gloom as cheer.

But there are moments when the proportions are perfect, and when we sit on our porches and listen to exactly the right amount of the right kind of rain cultivating our gardens in the best of all possible worlds.

We purr with contentment and approval; we smile inwardly and outwardly; we salute the excellent discretion of the elements; we can think of nothing finer than exactly what we are having.

There was such a blissful period late yesterday afternoon. A widely spaced sun-tinted rain began falling. As it seemed about to pass on toward Bolton, there was a sudden thickening of the sky, and the light rain turned into a sweet perpendicular drench. When this seemed to ease, there was a comfortable, far-off sound of thunder, and the sky thickened again and the good soaking proceeded.

There was no deviation from the straight-as-a-string fall of each drop, no blast of wind, no pelting of gardens, and any plants that quivered and danced in this rain were doing so from sheer joy of reaching out for assured life.

When it was all over, in the dusk, the world grew quiet, and the birds were still, except for a chorus of thrushes, as liquid and cool as the rain.

Handkerchiefs on the Lawn

There is no search for knowledge which time and patience and a little luck will not reward eventually.

For these long years we have been seeking a valid, authoritative, factual explanation of those cobwebs on the lawn which proclaim the coming of a hot sun, under which, when it comes, they fold and vanish.

We have pondered, without rescue from any friendly naturalist, whether some insect played a part in their creation, and if so, what insect, and why the handiwork appeared only on certain mornings. And it is not often that such pondering goes completely unrewarded for so many, many years. To tell the truth, the cobwebs had become, like any unresolved mystery, an annoyance, to the exclusion of easy contemplation of their natural and sparkling gossamer beauty.

But now, by that kind of chance that is no chance at all but the inevitable answer to long quest, we have come upon the information we wished. We have just read that Mr. Thoreau, in his time, was faced with the same question, in the curiosity of a little girl, and answered, promptly and authoritatively, from his unequaled knowledge of nature, that the cobweb was a handkerchief dropped by a fairy.

Rain and Cloud

Living under rain and cloud this spring and early summer has proved difficult for some drought-trained generations of suburban things and impossible for others. Tent caterpillars have failed to make it at all in many districts where they normally strip wild cherry, growing in its long hedgerows, down to black tree ghosts; some unfavorable chemistry of May cold and wet blighted the egg masses just in time.

Friendly things, too, have been hurt; the plight of tanagers, beaten down to city lawns by the cold weather and the consequent lack of insects, has been given lengthy public notice. There have been short, sad tales—relayed in that casual manner with which society treats everything relating to the robin—of young robins blown out of their nests by northeasters.

And the habitat of human beings has not been immune. The ground below has again become an invisible river for the rise and flow of water; householders have been startled to hear, in some vague cellarward region, the sigh and clang of rusted sump pumps being summoned out of their long drought-induced idleness. Germination has been uncertain in undersunned gardens, and first growth reluctant. The season has been running behind its calendar. Apple blossoms were late enough for hummingbirds; strawberries were late for their own festivals.

For these long years we have been seeking a valid, authoritative, factual explanation of those cobwebs on the lawn which proclaim the coming of a hot sun, under which, when it comes, they fold and vanish.

We have pondered, without rescue from any friendly naturalist, whether some insect played a part in their creation, and if so, what insect, and why the handiwork appeared only on certain mornings. And it is not often that such pondering goes completely unrewarded for so many, many years. To tell the truth, the cobwebs had become, like any unresolved mystery, an annoyance, to the exclusion of easy contemplation of their natural and sparkling gossamer beauty.

But now, by that kind of chance that is no chance at all but the inevitable answer to long quest, we have come upon the information we wished. We have just read that Mr. Thoreau, in his time, was faced with the same question, in the curiosity of a little girl, and answered, promptly and authoritatively, from his unequaled knowledge of nature, that the cobweb was a handkerchief dropped by a fairy.

Rain and Cloud

Living under rain and cloud this spring and early summer has proved difficult for some drought-trained generations of suburban things and impossible for others. Tent caterpillars have failed to make it at all in many districts where they normally strip wild cherry, growing in its long hedgerows, down to black tree ghosts; some unfavorable chemistry of May cold and wet blighted the egg masses just in time.

Friendly things, too, have been hurt; the plight of tanagers, beaten down to city lawns by the cold weather and the consequent lack of insects, has been given lengthy public notice. There have been short, sad tales—relayed in that casual manner with which society treats everything relating to the robin—of young robins blown out of their nests by northeasters.

And the habitat of human beings has not been immune. The ground below has again become an invisible river for the rise and flow of water; householders have been startled to hear, in some vague cellarward region, the sigh and clang of rusted sump pumps being summoned out of their long drought-induced idleness. Germination has been uncertain in undersunned gardens, and first growth reluctant. The season has been running behind its calendar. Apple blossoms were late enough for hummingbirds; strawberries were late for their own festivals.

Staremate

We have discovered, in our casual summer glimpses of the countryside, that this is a year in which flowers are craning over fences at us, rather than vice versa, and the handiest explanation is that this year's weather in the Northeast—an abnormally dry April, during which roots had to forage widely for moisture, followed by the heaviest May rainfall of several seasons—has been such as to produce an unusual legginess in plant growth.

The tall meadow rue, which has a normal capacity for growing taller than anything in its vicinity, has set new records; buttercups, in their June season, were spread high across the pastures; Queen Anne's lace, when it made its appearance early in July, unfurled its white parasols on stems that looked perilously long and languid. From the present height of the flowers, we can tell that the milkweed-pod explosions of next autumn are going to seem more like tufts of cloud than like anything grown from the earth. We are still in doubt about the eventual height of some of those sixty varieties of goldenrod whose blooms are likely to come under our inspection later on, but we are betting they will grow closer to the sun than before.

Only the vervain, normally the tallest of the summer herbs, has been holding back, as if it were still spent from its exertions last year, when it seemed extraordinary both for its height and for its blue density. Otherwise, this season's reach for sky has spread beyond the flowers of the fields and roadsides. There have been complaints about supposedly safely domesticated rosebushes that have suddenly shot illogical, suckerlike plumes toward the heavens, and about tomato vines starting out as if they would rather climb than bear. As for yucca, yucca blooms float so far above the lawns that they seem to have been cut free by a careless swipe of the plant's own sword-like leaves clustered below. No lifetime ever sees one year with roadsides and fields and fences and gardens exactly like those of another.

The Blast of the Sun

The formula we recommend for an interval of real hot weather is, of course, a mint julep, perpetually replenished, located in a shady breeze. Follow this formula faithfully, and soon you will never know there is a hot spell, or a freezing spell, or anything else.

Enjoyable and healthy as it may be, however, it is not the way to deal honestly with a heat wave. One should turn toward it, and face into it.

Out where the heat really thickens, the blade-leaf on the corn begins to curl and parch. The patch on the lawn spreads, as you watch it, like a spilled brown liquid. Something is drinking great gulps of the pond. Only the stiff, dry mechanism of the grasshopper seems to hold life in the meadow grass.

Yet, out under this heat-lamp sun, on the broiling landscape, where even the green things wilt soft and mutely desperate, one comes in touch with something that is splendor, as intoxicating in its own excessful way as a round of mint juleps, and more memorable.

This is the earth, Icarus-like, flying too close to its own great benefactor, and if the wings of our spirit melt off and plunge us dizzily down, until we feel faint and lost and close to nothingness, as if something final and oppressive were about to close over us, there was, in the moment before this, that feeling of near-union with something ultimate which our spirit is always seeking, against its own fears and timidity. Before the julep, frosty in the shade, take the blast of the sun.

Evening of the Giant Sheep

One evening a summer there comes a display of thunderheads marching and jousting across the sky. From black or gray base, the cloud mass tumbles itself up and up until, at last, it breaks out into the upper sunshine, fleece-white and soft and pure.

Once the sun finds this high target, which seemingly takes no color except the purest white, it will often spill its surplus colors down to the middle reaches of cloud, pinks and mauves as pure and spectacular as the white. Come dusk, the cloud masses will play ponderous hide-and-seek with a star, and, at their own summits, provide delicate, soundless wisps of lightning, from crag to crag. Between the white peaks, the sky is clean and blue.

The giant sheep tumble and frisk about, in their high pasture, until the world tires of counting them.

☙❦❧

Between Times

This is, without strict reference to the astrological calendar, our summer solstice, in which we sense the countryside lying peaceful and static between a time of effort and a time of fruitfulness.

It arrives, annually, when haying is done, and the early corn is ripe, and even the late corn grown up beyond the need of hoe. Like the occasional rainy day that gives the farmer a holiday when he himself wouldn't take it no matter how much he might need it, this is an interval in which the farmer is temporarily his own master. Behind him is the feverish struggle against time and soil and weed, and before him lies the inexorable labor of harvest. But for this present solstice, his fields and his crops are in order, his mow is full, the future holds its own worries.

This was the season when a farm boy could propose a day's fishing with the most confidence the proposal would be accepted and the fishing shared. It was, too, the season when country congregations held their annual church picnic, back in the days when Putnam Park and Lake Quassapaug were far off wonderlands suddenly made possible by the miracle of the automobile.

It was the season when a day's fishing or a joyous picnic might prey on the farmer's conscience so much he planned that the very next day he would undertake that most heartless of all summer tasks, brush cutting and fence trimming. But that was offense against the real spirit of the time. And that spirit, then as now, was one of blessed interlude, in which muscle knew it had earned the right to stretch and relax.

These are the days Connecticut is now having, and if Connecticut people have changed their habits, nature hasn't, and they need only pause to sense the solstice, all about them.

A few nights ago, the late-rising moon found a fine, upstanding mist waiting for it in the meadow. This mist added its own easy magic and transformed all outdoors into a shimmering fairyland neither landscape nor cloud, too beautiful and delicate to be altogether real, too peopled with shapes and imaginations to be just nothing but mist and moon and field. We heard a raspy locust tuning up in the pit, and soon we saw the characters assembling. We stood against the window, watching the performance through.

There were Oberon and Titania, and prankish Puck, and Cobweb, Moth and Mustardseed, and Pyramus and Thisbe, and Quince and Bottom and Flute, and a Wall for Pyramus and Thisbe to woo through, and even Moonshine produced both his thorn bush and his dog, all in as perfect and lightsome a rendering of *A Midsummer Night's Dream* as the Bard himself would have imagined, had he known such a midnight in Connecticut summer solstice.

Almanac

One evening early this month of August, we were privileged to hear a joint presentation of the summer song of the thrush and the fall fiddling of the katydid. We are told that it is not unusual for these two musical halves of the season to overlap; it often happens that a thrush will sing late or some katydid rehearse early.

But this year there was that single evening on which we heard the very last of the song that denotes the fullness of summer and the very first stirrings of the insect that is supposedly the prophet of frost to come within six weeks. And this, according friends of ours who make something of such notations and who also observed that the thrush remained silent on succeeding evenings, was an unusually precise timing for the changing of the musical guard.

The deep, falling tones of the thrush, coming always from a distance, as if they were being struck on bells hung in the wood, made us wish, now that it was getting too late, that we had spent a great deal more time in all the churches of summer. As for the katydid, sounding brisk and cheerful from a closer spot, near the roses, it named September 20 as the likely date for the first frost.

Hellgrammiting

This August heat suggests that we ought to use our memory to go hellgrammiting, the coolest possible thing to do in a summer world.

In the first place, the brook, a swift runner, had long since cut itself a deep and sheltered ravine, into which no sun penetrated. And the water, fresh from the spring-fed lake where the hellgrammites would be used, a little later on, was cool. The banks were cool, the water was cool, the air was cool, the stones over which the water flowed and under which the hellgrammites lodged were cool. An old pair of shoes, to guard against the sharper stones on the brook bed, let the cool water run through our toes. It took the continual plunging of one arm or the other to dislodge the stones. The hellgrammites were ugly cool, and the bait box, grass-bedded, was cool for them. When we think that a hellgrammite spends three years in the brook, before emerging to Dobson fly away, we think he has one of the coolest existences on record. Just how cool it is, under that spring-fed rush over stones, is something to dwell upon. He, fortunate fellow, dwells *in* it.

Well, as we were musing, there we were, decades ago, in that cool ravine, plucking the stones in the spring-fed water, getting ready to go fishing for the smallmouth in the cool, cool dawn, on the spring-fed lake, with just a little touch of fever over the bass, waiting so cool, down near the springs in the deep, deep bottom of the lake that fed the brook.

August Night

The Toscaninis of the August night are never podium-bound. They leap from thicket to thicket, from the brocaded shadow of the elm to the bright spotlight of the young maple standing clear in the moon. There is so much melody for them to lead, they grow careless of their time; let them drop a beat or two and it goes on without them, the most irrepressible and buoyant and joyous of all symphonies.

What personnel in the pit! Old and tried fiddlers, scraping their bows with the nonchalant assurance of at least two weeks of practice, and brash newcomers, who have no doubt of making the orchestra with their first faltering notes! Subdued flutists from their night shelter in the elderberry hedge, and big bass viol and horn, both from the same performer down in the shrinking pond! And then the deep-grass hummers, with the most self-assured monotones in all sound, and the high-branch percussionists with their free-style punctuations like the hepcat accompaniment to a swing session, and finally the Panhellenic chorus of thousands of crickets chirping in a brooding, fateful background to the fullness-of-summer theme.

It is the most indefatigable of symphonies. The hotter the night, the more sweltering the pit, the more zealous the performance. And even though it sometimes sounds and surges like a fever, it ends up, always, playing everything else to sleep.

Reprieve

From an early hour Sunday morning, as the strong wind from the south linked itself into the heat of the sun, the atmosphere was one of death. Not all the heat that had gone before, with its direct burning, seemed to have done the damage, the mortal injury, this incessant blowing threatened. Gardens shriveled and yellowed and wilted before the eye. The brown on the lawns was a moving thing. Trees gasped for a different kind of air. Butterflies danced what seemed the dance of death, the last feverish, aimless dalliance just before doom. There is nothing to drive a mood home, deep, like wind. And this day the mood was one of murder, premeditated, on the whole sweet body of summer.

All day the wind blew hot and strong from the south, until, at last, thin mutterings came from the west. And as the mutterings grew more distinct and close, it seemed that another head of death was shaping there—the dark head of furious onslaught, in contrast with the copperhead uncoiling from the south, but still, seemingly, its ally, yearning to complete its work, merciful only in that it promised to be sudden and complete in its strike.

The black death in the west grew blacker, and massed nearer, and came swirling across the fields, an angry cloud of dust riding before it, the anvils of doom ringing incessantly behind its curtain, the sparks flashing, the earth poised, still and trembling as if for some kind of last moment.

And then, in the instant of furious strike, the quick-dawning, illogical, out-of-character touch of mercy—the great wind not there, the ripping hail not there, the rain softening, the anvil clangor passing, the corn reviving, the garden soaking, the trees freshening, the heart lifting, and summer spared.

Hymn to the Aster

When the aster comes, we think there has been nothing before it, and nothing to come after. Here is the one completely satisfying reason why the sun began to grow warm in March, and why the clouds of April showed color, and why the rains came to fend off drought.

The aster gives lessons in geometry and in color. It is always the perfect circle, its radii curling in disciplined artistry toward, but never beyond, the compass line.

Until it blooms there has been no pure white, there has been no pure pink, there has been no royal purple.

When it blooms the eye knows it rests upon colors that will never be reproduced, except by another aster.

Home-Garden Summer

The soil itself is hard to please, and we, as its amanuensis, seem to spend many years chronicling small tomatoes and small potatoes, results common to either kind of weather extreme, flood or drought. In one year, when it rained all the time, we bewailed the fact that, although the professional farmers, who do everything scientifically, are able to counter drought by irrigation, they have as yet invented or produced no sun machines to run up and down their rows steaming off excess rain and thus correcting the irregular patterns of growth set into their plants by too frequent sluicings.

In another season, when it almost didn't rain at all, we found that only one crop seemed "happy"—as the flower growers say of their charges—under conditions of drought. The eggplant, a year-after-year problem for many who prize the purple-gloss beauty of the fruit even more than they like to eat it, flourished sturdily in its rows, produced blossoms close to the earth, and soon leaned on its own fruit. The only other noticeable direct beneficiary of drought was purslane, the weed once boiled up for greens or used in salads. Purslane seeds itself and roots itself with little moisture, refuses to die as long as it is left in any kind of contact with soil, and roots anew from every last shred of itself when it is chopped up with a hoe. Apparently, as soon as the Puritan settlers could afford to without going hungry, they rejected purslane as a table vegetable. Anything so easily come by could not possibly be good for us.

This year it is a pleasure to be able to write, after so many years of tilted weather and cycled crop fortunes, of a home-garden summer that has not been too cool or too hot, too dry or too wet, but, to judge by the quality and quantity of its produce, just right.

This has been a season in which the humblest vegetable patch in the countryside hereabouts could produce peas that tasted as if they had been grown in France, when carrots came out of the ground early, in uniform size and untwisted shape, as if they had been intended to be props for a still-life painting, and when the crispness in the sink of successive crops of string beans made housewives remember again that they are also called snap beans. Tomatoes on early hybrid vines provided thick, quick-ripening clusters of moderate-size fruit; at midseason, inside the deeper foliage of the old standbys, half- to three-quarter-pound green globes began turning yellow and pink and red. Bibb lettuce, which is slowly continuing its conquest of the gardens of the East, folded large, shell-like leaf on leaf and made big heads without bolting. Peppers crowded together in the center of their bush, handsome in size, uniform, glossy.

Cucumber vines produced before they wandered far. Each

clump of squash rose quickly to create and shade its own tropical interior world, with chasms of light in which the yellow of summer sun and summer crookneck were mixed. Sweet onions swelled out to the circumference of a hamburger. Corn and lima beans grew on the same schedule. There was nothing one could ask for that was not there.

Lost Piece of Sky

The office mariner, whose knowledge is presumably authentic, described the passage over Manchester yesterday morning of an opening of sun and blue sky, followed by more scudding clouds, as the "eye" of our waning hurricane. It was, he said, the calm, deceptively placid center, carried along inside the whirling force of the storm.

Leaving technical terms and expert hurricanology aside, there was one thing we observed as an amateur. It was that that patch of sunlight and blue sky was not of New England. The sky was still carrying the reflection of bluer waters than we know. The light clouds that fringed this blue were still palm-brushed. The whole opening, in the midst of the storm, moved in one piece as if it had been carried intact from its first Caribbean origin all the way across Florida and back again and up the coast to Manchester. And shortly after this "eye" had passed, there was a flight of strange sea birds past our window, beating its way back south against the new, but now more fitful, rush of wind.

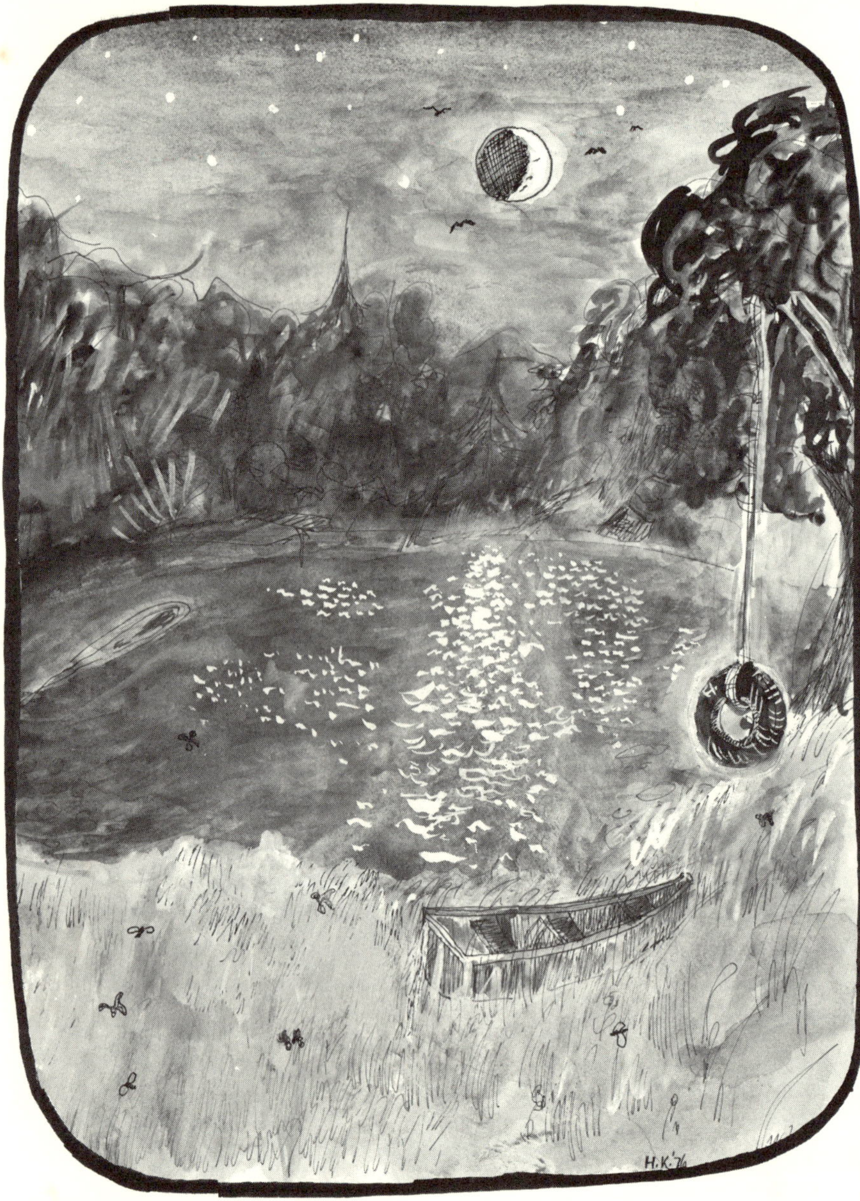

In the Twilight

As the sun sinks, these misty evenings, there establishes itself, between earth and sky, the world of the ghostly things to whom the twilight, and the twilight alone, is freedom.

Unless it is a heron or bittern materializing out of the mist to take a night perch over the pond, there is no way of knowing what manner of wings flutter and beat and glide their way through the kindly yet mysterious gloom.

Nor, unless a corner of moonlight or starlight happens to strike its path, is there any certainty about what moves and ripples the water below. It may be something occasionally seen in daylight—a giant frog, a fat, lazy trout, or a muskrat—and it may be something never seen, completely protected in its anonymity because it moves only in this twilight zone.

These mysterious movements in air and water are mist-screened against our precise knowledge of them, and yet, behind that protection, they come breathlessly near the senses, at once almost unreal and overpoweringly present. Their world and their time are their own, and their perceptions and instincts lead them on a course of life completely foreign to ours, and yet there are these half-light moments when the two worlds brush against each other, and none can know which is the more real.

Beyond Neuroses

Many signs have been pointing to this as the year in which the single-minded forms of life—the insects—could be getting ready to take over.

It goes back to May, in the morning of the season, when gnats clouded the air, and it seems to be ending now with an unparalleled indoor invasion of crickets claiming to themselves a share of the closed-season warmth and cheer of the television room. In between, Japanese beetles returned in force to the rose gardens, taking over from hordes of chafers. An unidentified succession of moths covered the nighttime window screens. Locusts turned the noons drowsy, and katydids the moons. Gypsy moths gyrated in egg-laying orgies in new areas, many miles from the scenes of this year's defoliations.

The yellowjackets of September hovered over the warmth of picnics, or any other outdoor sociability, in the middle of August. Among all these notable survivors this season, a small, round, dark breed of spider seemed likely to be *the* form of life best equipped for survival. It inhabits the tubes and crannies of metal lawn furniture, or the concrete of patios, is agile beyond the reach of any spray, and living without visible web or obvious organic prey, seems capable of making both home and diet of the same metal-and-concrete complex we human beings have evolved as our prime environment.

The more one watches the world of small creatures, the more grimly one is impressed by the way its populations seem to be programmed beyond neurosis to do the unquestioned thing unquestioningly, with no free will, no conscience, no out-of-reach dreams, no anticipation of success or failure, no grim indulgence in play as they go along, to flaw their compliance.

As a Summer Ends

For the calendar, and for some lucky people, summer ends this evening.

The unlucky ones are those for whom summer was ending, in their thoughts, even as it began.

We, the unlucky ones, are cursed with the capacity to see the ending in every beginning. It is one of the dismal faculties some people develop after they first discover their own personal time is constantly accelerating. Later on, if they turn lucky, they are blessed again, not with the blessing of childhood, which is that each moment can seem eternal and complete for itself, but with the blessing of wisdom and philosophy, which can conquer even the foreordained passing of a precious thing, like a summer.

But between the innocence of childhood and the saddened, richer wisdom of age, there is indeed a wasteland, where one sees the death of a summer even in its birth, and rages against its going even as one thrills to its coming, and lives every second of it with a poisoned, futile concentration, so afraid of losing it that one never freely enjoys it.

Once it did not matter, the passing of a summer, and now it matters too much. Later on, perhaps, it will be a more peaceful and pleasant part of the rich order of things.

Even in this interim discontent of summers, when childhood refuses to return, we begin to see that we live each one differently, that each has its own unique and passing mood. And we discover, when the time for farewell comes, that we have loved each summer not because it was pure repetition, but because it has added its own touch to the composite recollection and anticipation provided by all our summers.

So a summer ends, this evening, as summer ended a thousand years ago, for whatever and whoever was sentient then, and as summers will end for the children of children, and we have almost, but not quite, written the pang out of it.

Yellows

Even the name of the month has its color connotation. Look at the word September lazily, receptively, and you will notice the word itself taking on a yellowish tinge. It is the month of yellows.

You can go about the countryside, through the fields, and make yellow the continuity of your walk. It is yellow-rod saluting you, or the pumpkin gleaming, or the Bartlett ripening, or the single leaf that can't wait for what will now come soon enough for all. It is the cornfield past picking, and the wiry fall dandelion, and the drought patch on the lawn. And it is the month of the yellowest sun.

It is the month of yellow things that sting. The jeweled ugliness of the yellow spider is pinging its web violently at every turn. And hornets, sometimes angry merely at a presence or a sound, are omnipresent, reckless, insistent, underfoot, on every blossom, buzzing every square inch of every kind of space, and acting as if, having inherited the earth, they intend to sting it to death.

This is the cruel side of yellow and September, which sets the tone for the month, and for the beauty of things in the last stage of fruitfulness. It is a month that makes ready for death.

Where is its solace, then? Well, it puts on airs that beguile us away from its mortal assault upon summer, and it makes almost every dawn a fairyland of sun and mists, and the stars never march more gloriously behind a young moon, and as the month wears on the whirl of the stingers fades and there is peace, a peace of completion.

The Postscript Splendor

> Here come the flowers,
> Here come the grasses,
> Here comes September,
> We hail her as she passes.

This old New England processional song and autumnal chant, so full of simple, classic charm as the harvesters of wild asters and goldenrod and everlasting let it keep homeward step for them, will serve here for our little processional past summer and toward autumn.

September's beauty comes as the earth, having fulfilled its utilitarian functions and carried out its good cooperation with the husbandry of men, suddenly gives itself completely over to one last wanton burst of bloom that has no higher purpose than to delight the eye and sky. Patches of the goldenrod and purple aster, rising through morning mist, peaceful friends to the noonday sun, flinging their colors against the western twilight, represent art for art's sake and have no point except that of beauty itself.

There comes a time when the human processional, which marches with such pure seasonal festiveness down the reaches of this postscript splendor, is shadowed overhead by the march of low gray clouds propelled by a wind that has cool resources, and will be the coming of autumn.

The Time of the Spider

All beautiful summer long, nothing has seemed so pure as the sun and the dew and the air, and nothing so sweet and healthful as the growth on the land.

Yet from such seeming purities and sweetnesses there was gradually being distilled and accumulated and concentrated, all the beautiful summer long, the sac of poison that is the body of the yellow spider.

The spider's embodiment of evil hangs heavy, but all too nimble, these September days, at garden's edge, in shrub corner, across woodland path, and the eye and sense accustomed to placid summer beauty, to summer peace, recoil sharply from its vivid threat, the threat of ugliness so concentrated it has become like a jewel.

Where was this poison, to be distilled from summer? Where in the grasses, the winds, the dews? Where did these evils lurk, beneath the fairness of a summer day? We might have sworn they were not there. How could there be the raw materials of venom in the world of the clover and the wild rose?

They were there, as their September embodiment reveals. And now they have come into their own, poised vibrantly just where our hand would like to reach for one more summer flower. Sure-footed on their webs, they hang like globules of bottled sunlight, blocking our path and confusing our late-summer mind into pretentious thoughts of good and evil.

On This September Air

We were sitting at our office window, dreaming our business, when an indescribable fragrance, seemingly off Main Street itself, came in the window.

That evening, in more rural surroundings, the fragrance rose again. This time it seemed to float in over the western hills, washing gently in the meadow, stirring through the goldenrod.

The next morning, in the cornfield, there was the same fragrance again.

It was heavy and almost tropical, like the air outside a lotus garden, and it had a musk short of the open sweetness of new-mown hay, and it suggested, faintly, distant groves of peaches and festoons of grapes, and dropping apples, and fields of grain that might be lending something to the wind, and yet most certainly was none of these alone.

But since we had found it within a range of several miles, and it seemed free upon a whole succession of airs, we had to conclude that something in the September combination of waning sun and increased humidity released vapors a stronger sun or an earth more parched would have beaten down or imprisoned and that the fragrance was indeed a distillation of all the things it suggested—of the late flowers in the meadows and the low, matted tangle of the half-rotted undergrowth, of the turning grape and of the falling apple and of the ragweed and the breath of the trees and the September rose and of the ripe brown body of Autumn herself.

A Lady Not to Be Denied

Exactly three hours before the scheduled time, autumn sent her heralds and outriders scurrying across the sky. They were black, tumbling, swiftly maneuvering clouds, carried by winds so high they did not yet disturb a leaf. Scudding, scouring, crisscrossing each other into every lair of mist and rain and humidity, they swept the air clean, suddenly swooped down and stripped from the ash a triumphal carpet of leaves, and then passed on, leaving the way open for the sun to slant down with the last drying and tidying touches. For a brief span, then, there was the last illusion of summer.

Soon after three o'clock, the lady herself appeared, riding a cool, clear wind and a light fringe of sea-shell-tinted clouds, reaching possessively down, now and then, to stroke the blushing and adoring sumac, rippling her fingers across the pond and grass, blowing a cool kiss to the wild, white asters, and signaling majestically, to lowly humans, her proud command of limitless armies raised in western and Arctic fastnesses and already on the move relentlessly, to confirm her expanding sovereignty.

It was no contradiction of terms, but rather a rare and perfect union of opposites, to call the ensuing surrender both unconditional and exhilarating.

❦

Nocturne

When summer comes back to a young harvest moon, and the evening is warm again and full of lavish airs, there are emergency things to be done, and no waiting on them.

It is important to note that one evening the air is clear and still, stars in the sky with the half moon, the shadows sharp and distinct, and that then, the next evening, haze hides the companion stars, all but a strong few, and softens the lines of the shadows, and mellows the face of the moon itself, while winds are veering more strongly from the south.

It is important to see how the winds, on this second evening, lift and toss and weave the pendant branches of the elm, until a New England greenery, which is perhaps browned and beetled by light of day, wears all the lush richness and mystery and romance of the tropics.

It is important to hear what music the winds play through the giant ash, with what steady and insistent sighings the wind loves.

It is important to trace, from one evening to another, the later rising and change of arc in the moon itself, the sad, inevitable cycle in which it monitors and reflects our sequences of fruition, fullness, and passing.

Yes, when summer comes back to a young harvest moon, and the evening is warm and full of lavish airs, not a moment should be lost, nor nuance of shadow, nor least play of wind in any corner of fairyland, nor least turn of beloved face.

Queen of the Evening

In a week of softly changing colors, of vistas subtly more beautiful each succeeding day, it has been a special power of the ash that has most engaged our wonder and affection.

The lemon drop of the birch, the scarlet of the oak, the red rage of the maple—these hold the daylight hours, resplendent as they face the sun. And during their hours of glory the massive high-crowned ash, like a dull and unimaginative maiden aunt, seems rather out of it, wearing a sober gown of brown, capturing no eye, seeming to be the most prosaic figure in the countryside procession.

Then the sun dips, so low it no longer fingers the early evening planes, and the dusk advances. All the daytime bursts of brilliance have vanished. But just as the color addict feels free to go indoors, the display over, the darkness is beaten back one last time by a surprise auburn glow from the ash, a massive incandescence that is no reflection, or no mere surface appearance, but an inner life of light pouring itself out through the foliage, like a great Japanese lantern.

How the ash stores this light, behind its dull daytime exterior, in which it hardly seemed to be taking the sun, and then gives it back to dusk, long after the sun has gone, how the daytime maiden aunt happens to become the lustrous queen of the evening, it is not within our province to know. This much wisdom has been gained: never call an early October evening finished until the ash, too, has finally flickered out.

Raspberries on the Lawn

On Main Street, a few doors from the Griswold Inn in Essex, Connecticut, as October drew to a close, a weigela bush was in full bloom. In Salisbury, across Route 44 from the Town Hall, an impromptu picnic-lunch party had fresh-picked raspberries set out in dishes on the lawn. In a hillside garden in nearby Cornwall, a tower of Van Doren morning glories defied the mild October sun and stayed open late into the afternoon.

Elsewhere in Connecticut there were the second bloomings, the oddities, the persistencies and confusions of a season prolonging itself beyond its natural time. A yellow day lily shot up out of its supposed dormancy and budded. In vegetable gardens, Kentucky Wonder beans continued their yield; tomato vines, once exhausted, began to blossom and set again; little green peppers reappeared; pumpkin vines that had already oversupplied the roadside stands began making new green pumpkins; rose gardens that had produced bonus surges for August and September came out with candelabra arrays of new buds and blooms, shoulder high.

Confused by such unusual traffic signals, the migrating fall warblers loitered along the route, crowding the thickets. In Hartford County, an unexpected stopping-over of mockingbirds jammed the airwaves with disjointed, frantic mimicry and catapult dances of spring courtship. Only the stars, with the nightly earlier appearance of Orion wheeling evenly on toward November, seemed to be keeping the true season.

All Over Again, Taped

Sitting out the other afternoon, we heard the spring peepers, persisting in a frost-rimmed swamp. Overhead, wheeling, as if they had not yet decided what reeds to come down to for a summer of feeding and breeding, were twenty or thirty redwinged blackbirds, who had gone back to the "coo-ee" calls typical of blackbirds at their spring arrival.

From a leafless aspen beside the swamp, robins produced, in the dry, clear October air, the same especially melodic notes that robins, every spring, seem to pipe through rain before they finally release them. There was even one earnest, dedicated robin who appeared to be lining an old nest. Over all, a meadowlark sang, high and irrepressible—again, as in spring.

One thinks one could never have enough of summer until, in some grotesque flip of the weather in October or November, blackbird, peeper, robin, and meadowlark commit the cruel indiscretion of threatening to give it to us all over again, taped.

Even Flowers Were Tired

Enough is indeed enough. Even the flowers, living straight and beautiful the way we all would like to, were tired.

Tired, too, were the trees waiting a chance to let their foliage fall. Tired the lawns, tired the gardens, with squash leaves still green in late October, tired the birds waiting for final word to head south.

All these, and that part of us which is part of them, were waiting for release. And when it came—a sprinkle of dew gripped, as soon as it fell, by the icy look of the stars—nothing really shivered or trembled or asked for stay. Everything took the ice, deep into its heart, and then waited for the sun, the giver of life, to reach down and take back its gift. To whom else should it be rendered back?

We walked out in this willing death, and turned to watch the moon drifting through the now skeletoned ash, and traitor ourselves to the summer we love above all seasons, thought we had never seen anything of such pure beauty as that chill geometry.

In New England, every season woos, and wins.

The Burning of Leaves

The burning of leaves—a relatively innocent offender—will have come under complete control in this country long before any of the other pollutants of our air have been properly dealt with. This, aside from the obvious aesthetic deprivations it entails, uncovers the weak side of all crusading that makes a big show while it attacks the gentlest, least offensive enemy first, and leaves the real villains for some unnamed date.

When one examines the methods of leaf control being employed to avoid the traditional burning—the municipalities that still have trees run their public works collection equipment on regular leaf-pickup schedules, and home owners are beginning to prepare their leaf crops for town collection by driving leaf-vacuuming machines up and down their lawns—one sees the possibility that the various motors employed in collecting and transporting the leaves may pollute the neighborhood air as much as the burning itself might have done.

But if leaf control has to come, and come before we try society's power against exhaust pipes, diesel plumes, and smokestacks, we would like it down on the record that during the exceptionally long leaf season just closed we were able to spend one Sunday-morning hour at a window that looked out on a late-leaved maple.

The only visible thing happening to the tree was that the warm rising sun was fingering its way through the foliage. No breath of air was stirring. In this complete but warming

Sabbath calm there came, from high in the tree, the movement of a leaf disengaged and tumbling down, in unpredictable and erratic directions dictated only by its own structural aerodynamics, until, having brushed against other leaves and turned away from branches, it came to its easy landing. Another fell, and another, and within the next hour, still with no puff of wind, no movement of air other than that caused by the falling leaves themselves, the tree, knowing its own time, had slipped a pattern of scarlet and yellow down to the ground.

The Urge and the Fear

The beautifully ominous yellow spiders we have been watching have all disappeared. We still walk with a somewhat primeval fear past certain spots. But the webs are broken down and shattered, their intricate design of air and trap and alarm bedraggled into aimless chaos. The spiders grew fat, and beautiful, in their own way, and set about reproducing themselves, and then disappeared from the scene.

We did not witness the final exit of any one of them, but we can venture to reconstruct it. As he approached maturity, each male spider began to experience an urge and a fear. Both are basic and instinctive in every living thing. The urge was to perpetuate himself. The fear was of death.

For the spider, both are quite likely to come almost as one act, almost at one moment. That moment arrives when the male conquers his fear, leaves his own web, and goes to that of his fair lady. He twangs at the edge of her web, trembling in his combination of passion and dread, and hesitantly advances up the web to his happiness and his fate. At this point, he develops what some of our modern philosophers term "the courage to be," which is, perhaps, nothing more than the courage even to die fulfilling life. His lady loves him, and then, like as not, she eats him, just as he feared she would.

As for the fair lady, we like to believe she explodes of sentimental remorse, rather than of satiety and old age. But all that we non-spiders know, as we walk by the empty, tattered, and torn web, is that a fear in retrospect is almost as chilling as one based on anticipation. The spider, at least, faces it only once.

The Longest Season

Now at the entrance to November there is still an occasional Norway maple that has not yet dropped its leaves; the end has been so long delayed that one doesn't dare, even now, predate a final release.

It is already established, however, that the time span between bare branch in the spring and the same branch bare again in autumn has been remarkably long, possibly the longest ever known in Connecticut.

There have been some side-show oddities reflecting the unusually persistent renewal of vitality through the season, among them a transplanted shad-blow that first died and lost all leaves and then, in midsummer, suddenly leaved out a second time and continued a normal existence. One hard-luck apple branch claimed special notice. During the bitter January of last winter, squirrels famined by snow and cold had stripped it bare of much of its bark; it missed the first round of spring life, but by July had reknitted its bark well enough to push forth a few leaves. These soon formed the target for a web of caterpillars, who ate the branch bare again and then departed in their cycle. In September the still undiminished power of the season stirred the branch to activity once again, and this time it produced, at last, apple blossoms.

Such freakishness also has been noted in humbler plant forms. It has been a year of record height and vigor for mullein spikes, which, long after normal growth, several times renewed their yellow flowers and their skyward climb. The steady visits of humid weather, the timely arrival of rains, and, finally, the long abstention of killing frost, made possible the repeated resurgence of the summer life force, until it seemed that green growth would never end. There are some unpleasant incidental statistics. Five additional mowings of the lawn were necessary. The gin season required an extra case of tonic.

Each season practices its own individual evocations and repulsions. Wild morning glories, which had been strangling one corn patch for the past four years, made their appearance this year as usual, but then, at the moment when they normally twine their way up the cornstalk and around the ear, suddenly faded to nothingness, leaving the field clean.

The side lawn, one humid September day, spawned thousands of transparent pale-green worms, about two inches long, aimless in the grass, complete strangers one would be well pleased never to classify or see again. One suspected that had it not been for the peculiar chemistry of this particular season, they would never have lived at all. The earth must be full of strange life capable of waiting for the precise combination of air, sun, and rain which suddenly strikes a new cycle into its cells, or which stirs germination inside some long-dormant seed.

A season that could give so many weird calls to the unusual ended by mixing its signals for the birds. The myrtle warblers came down late—it was around the fifteenth of October when they first appeared—and then discovered that they were still too early, and their migration stacked up until they sometimes crowded the lawns as far as the windowsills. By the time they finally left, just the other day, they had finished off the bayberries that normally belong to the waxwings, who, incidentally, have not put in their appearance, even yet.

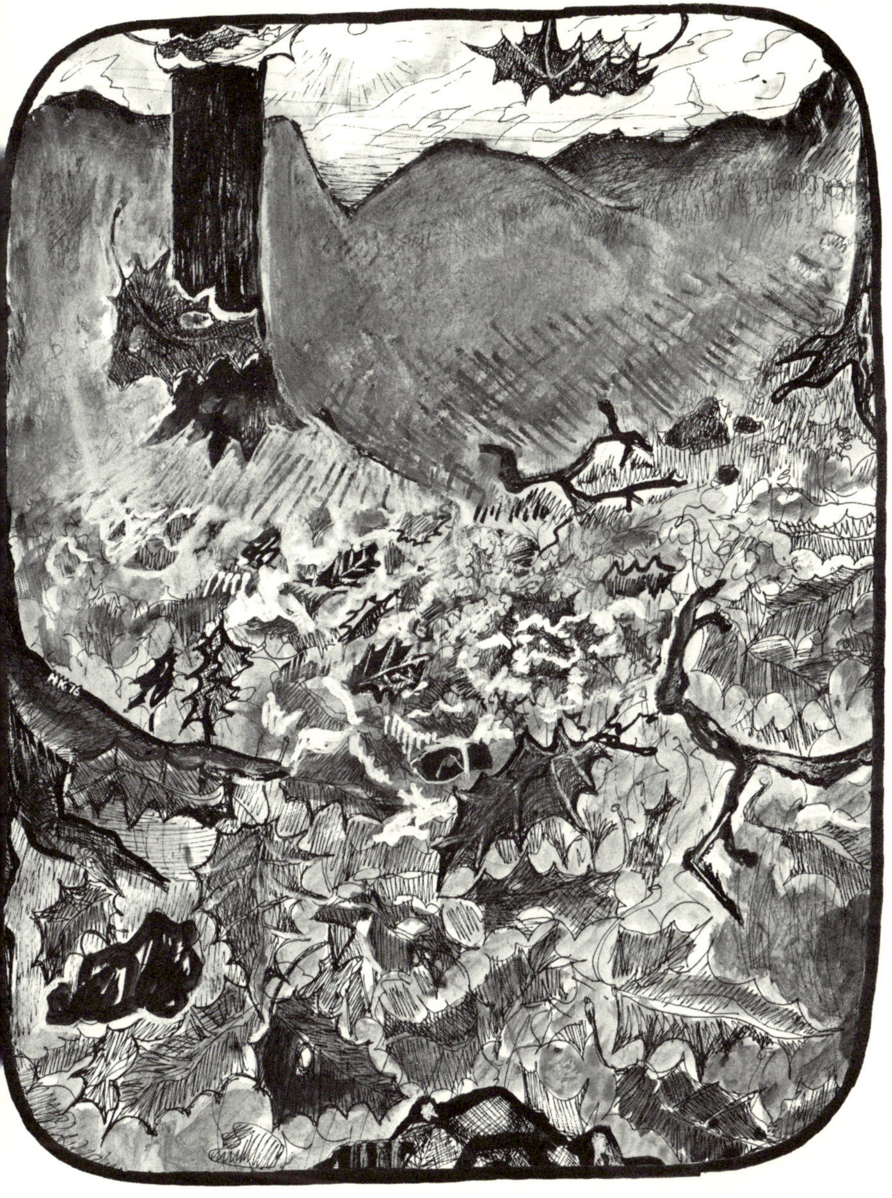

The Placid Turn

It is with a placid turn—an emphasis of its own quiet and tranquil moods—that November has opened.

Under the roof of morning mists, before the sun burns through, there is nothing that moves, and as the mist returns again at night, to cloak the wheeling beauty of the fall firmament, there is motionless silence again. It is as if all of earth, at last, had been calmed out of its fever and growth and struggle and yielded into a serenity of fulfillment.

The leaves lie where they drift down. The cattle drowse in the slanting sun. There should be, standing somewhere if the pasture were a complete pasture, at least one fringed gentian, most tranquil of blooms. If there were chestnuts, they would be dropping now, without a sound.

To the Quiet November Eye

The gaily pennoned green chivalry of the corn has been cut down to stubble, and the stubble retreats sadly across the fields of frost-moist brown earth.

The teeming white fruitfulness of the long green lines of potato vines has been gutted. The summer tobacco jungle hangs upside down in drafty barns as though it were the victim of some weird, aboriginal torture process.

The orchards are bare, the last red of the windfalls fading into a frozen brown rot. The pond has dipped below its grass edge, baring brown banks. The glare of the sumac has faded from the hill, and even the scrub oak has sobered after its long splash of October wine.

Yet if the landscape has turned sere, it seems to provide

the proper background for the spare whites and grays which would be noticed in no other season of the year.

With each succeeding frost, the bayberry on the side hill turns one more shade from gray toward white.

On the crest of the hill, the young birch thicket reaches at last its true birch heritage, setting a forest of slender white candles underneath the last flame of the four-o'clock sun.

This is also a time when the bark of great trees comes into its own, with its shy, luminous mosaic of grays tinged with every other soft color. There is a miniature pattern in a few square inches of such bark which offers, to the quiet November eye, a panorama of romantic journeying. It is a loveliness that has had to wait all a noisy color year long for attention, and that may escape you still, if you do not pause by a tree, as a friend.

The quiet, spare, yet elegant beauty of November in Connecticut does not flood toward you, or beat upon your senses with colorful demands for recognition. *You* must go toward *it*, with slow and friendly tread and lingering eye, and a heart ready to stand still for a flake.

On the Forest Floor

Underneath the spired silver of the forest top, the forest floor lies calm and still, hoarding its random pools of sunny warmth, unruffled by the cool north wind that whistles around the forest edges. Outside is autumn, and the fields yielding frost slowly to the morning sun. Here, inside the wood, the leaves all are down at last, each individual downward flight and destination the result of a new draw in an endless lottery. Like tickets cashed and spent, they make a friendly litter on the forest floor.

Yet their myriad chance had design and purpose; the blanket they laid is trim and snug for winter.

Winter, fall, and summer meet, and as the green that summer waved aloft has turned and fallen, winter has begun to show its own imperishable, hardier wares. They are presented close to earth, as exhibits with modest but enduring value. There is princess pine, the perfect miniature, wintergreen and rattlesnake plant, the running pine, the partridge berry with its shy wanderings by stone and twig, and the great Christmas fern that stays green all winter long.

◈

The Chickadee and the Jets

The months just ahead are those in which the bewitched legion of people who regard the chickadee primarily as a spirit will be deep in their annual love affair, and we find it a pleasant task to pass along to all such devotees what may be a new entry for their gospel.

Our section of suburbia is also jet territory. The other morning—whether it was the sheer exuberance of the fine fall weather up above or the military's way of calling the populace back to the facts, rather than the smiles, of international life— the peace of our landscape was disturbed by a frightening succession of sonic booms.

As one crackling report followed another, and the earth shook, and the windows rattled, a single set of earthly consternations kept repeating itself. The family dog ran for a dark hiding place. The sun-worshipping cats scattered crazily. Crows took off in sudden flight. Robins warned their full-grown young. Some caged pheasants croaked in terror. And we, representing the populace, obediently thought the inevitable thoughts: *This* was what man was doing to his world.

But each time, when the last echo had rumbled over the horizon, the next sound was the song of the chickadee, so regular, so undisturbed as to knit the morning air back together, just as if nothing had happened.

This cool behavior of the bird was sustained, with the same hushed-moment timing, the same nonchalance, the same emphasis on what the bird seemed to consider significant and valuable, through the whole series of sonic blasts. At last the military, having done what it felt it had to do, went down to lunch, and the chickadee, having pointed out what else must be done, flew out of the garden.

Now the Sun . . .

Now the sun is in the south for its rising and its setting, and the earth, growing cold, spins its bleak way farther and farther from its source of warmth and life. Yet against the cold spaces of the evening sky the smoke of the hearth fire writes its symbolism of man at reflective peace, and between the outer chill and the inner warmth of November the mood for appraisal and thanksgiving is created, so that custom merely follows the natural and inevitable instincts of New England and Connecticut living.

Were there no date marked upon the calendar, were there no rite of plumped bird, those who have lived the past season in any proximity to nature's bounty, who have spent a portion of their time in constructive communion with the good Connecticut soil, would still pause for a reverent and heart-stirred acknowledgment of the bond between man and his home acres.

The nature of that bond does not vary from year to year. There have been years in which the earth in its moods has been intractable, so that bitter desolation stood in the finest fields of

Connecticut. And there have been years, like this, in which the bounty of the soil seemed unlimited.

But the sense of being bound to the soil, be it for better or for worse, but being bound regardless, provides a basic philosophical dividend that no temporary vagaries of the terrain, in its half of the relationship, can materially alter.

That dividend would be certain in any year. But this has been a year of mellow wonder, a year in which the benevolent conspiracy of earth and nature has been most successful. From the first green seedlings of April to the last frost-spared yield of October, the smooth, even flow of fruitfulness spread triumphantly through Connecticut valleys and up Connecticut hillsides. Even the rains came always on time.

Now that flow of fruitfulness has ceased. Human husbandry has ended, and the wild seed is sown, and the earth lies resting from its prodigious labors.

But these spare fields, these now barren hillsides, this broad brown valley, and these irregular pastures nuzzling their way between silent sentinel wood lots, still breathe the richness and fullness of life itself, Connecticut version, to which it is a dear and irreplaceable privilege to belong.

Her Calendar

A friend of ours lives at the foot of a hill, from which she harvests, from season to season, the basic necessities of her kind of life.

In March, at the opening of her year, she climbs the hill through the soft thaw looking for pussy willows, which she arranges in a pewter pitcher underneath a mirror.

In May, apple blossoms replace the willows.

In October, for the next long-lease tenure of the place under the mirror, it is bayberry, clipped and trimmed and massed into a bluish-grayish-white cloud.

The other day, the climb was to cut laurel branches, which she arranges in window boxes to keep the exterior of her house bright while the uncandled bayberry gives the interior its incandescence.

We have a note from her, written after her expedition for the laurel, in which she describes walking in late-fall woods in rain. The rain, she says, seems to be putting the earth to sleep. With her, it is pussy willow time, bluet time, violet time, apple blossom time, lady's-slipper time, wild rose time, black-eyed Susan time, blackberry time, bittersweet time, maple leaf time, bayberry time, laurel time, from one year to the next.

Look from a Hill

From a hill with a view, reacquaintance with the landscape is now in order. The cluster of homes hidden all summer long, as deeply as though they were situated inside some forest primeval, now comes forward with bright paint and stain. The white church steeple, unshaded now, stands tall and isolated in its purest New England heritage. The far-off glint of windshields maps out cross-country roads no summer view could identify. A pond is blue and bare, that never answered summer sky.

And somehow, as the countryside loses its fastnesses, its camouflage, its privacies, distances shrink, and thoughts too, until the dominion of the eye becomes more of a community, more of a neighborhood, than ever in summer, when eye had to pause and leap and ponder and guess.

Knob and hill, valley and rise, stand at last in some geographical relationship to one another. One could risk, now, a cross-country journey, as the crow would fly it, and achieve and hold something of a crow's sense of direction. And the eye, at least, does make the journey, from neighborhood to neighborhood, and if the hill is high enough, from town to town, and county to county.

The Purest Form

Once again, as the snow provides the parchment background for bare outline of tree, we feel drawn to the purest poetry our world provides.

The green lyric traceries of spring, the lush odes of flowering summer, the rich stanzas of colored autumn, all yield, in the end, to the least adorned of poetry—that of the winter outline.

Here is proved, on landscape, what some already know from lines and figures on paper—that geometry is the purest form of poetry, which can inspire in the mind a beauty not dependent upon, or adulterated by, the more obvious enticements to the senses. Here, in this moment when the superficial observer, or the spirit too wedded to the outer foliage of beauty, might pronounce all beauty gone, there arrives the basic pattern upon which the soft alliterations of spring, the pulsing meters of summer, and the gaudy rhymes of fall are builded.

Here, before the heart and the senses are engaged, is the feast for the mind's eye, for those perceptions which are themselves as clean and bare and spare as the gray lines of a tree against winter white.

First of the Winter

When all the sky itself is a fragile globe of unbroken robin's egg blue, with the thin gold leaf of the departed sun curling its last edge over the horizon, and the earth is revolving whitely under a dusting of snow, you step out and see the first new moon of the winter.

It is the thinnest, most delicate of jewels, so light in its line that the eye, unable to trust its own judgment as to where the reality ends, completes the full circle until, in vision at least, there stands in the western sky the lightest closed crown twilight ever wore.

Only the clear cold brilliancy of the white earth and pastel sky, and the crystalline air between, could make this first trace of the first moon of the winter visible at all. In misty spring or hazy summer it would not have been seen until it was another night older.

Season's Greetings

After the winds and storms of autumn have lashed the trees to penitence, there sometimes comes a large-flaked and otherwise inconsequential snow which gives to the trees and their landscape the sequel gift of innocence. It was in such a landscape, on the morning of such a fall, that we began having our thoughts about the end of one year and the beginning of another. The snow seemed helpful, in that it blotted out the bright surface shapes of specific recollection in favor of the more enduring and powerfully molded impressions of fundamental structures and meanings, not always easy to see when one is in the midst of them, but finally, with luck and discernment, becoming clear and significant in the same way the height and outline of a mountain pass assert themselves for the first time after the transcontinental train has begun its leisurely descent.

In such a mood, we discovered that the year which is passing out behind us has done more for us, in the way of providing landmarks and definitions, than our querulous impatience has paused to consider. To the old eternal questions that keep pounding at us—what is man? who are we? why are we here?—there has, come to think of it, been more than one suggested answer. The answers point, perhaps, in the direction of something we have known all along, with our questioning less a search for knowledge or reassurance than a device for fending off the awesome involvement and responsibility we ought to assume and accept.

The involvement of being a leading actor and recorder in what has been created cannot be disregarded; the grandeur of the pattern receding and unfolding behind us does somehow include us. The continuing responsibility comes down to the least something we can do—which is the business of putting one foot ahead of the other even when we are uncertain and afraid.

There have been those moments in the past year when we knew what man was and who we were and why we were here. Our questions were answered often suddenly and unexpectedly, in the impact of a phrase in the midst of a reading, in the glimpse of a quick, unconscious communion of faces waiting for a light to change, in the discovery of the real presence of strength and serenity in the face above a clerical collar, in the bright holiday of sunlight when a President jokes about the jokes about himself, in a woman's arrangement of some flowers; in some flicker-lens moment when streets and buildings and sky seem fused into one infinite invitation for something in the breast to emerge and journey forward forever, and the journey seems winged even though if you were to look down you would still find one foot poking itself stolidly ahead of the other.

With the turn of the calendar, we are moving toward what the geophysicists are beginning to call the International Years of the Quiet Sun, which sound, in advance, as if they might be rich in recognitions and realizations. But if that is true, there will still not be much difference between time travel forward or backward, and so, while the soft snow clings to the branch, in a moment which may belong to both directions, season's greetings.

The Jolly Monarch

Because we have become a civilization so intent upon avoiding discomfort and inconvenience—so very intent upon avoiding them that we put ourselves to all kinds of discomfort and inconvenience in order to defeat and resist the influences of the changing seasons—most of us have adopted a harsh and unpleasant view of winter, considering it an enemy to be resisted and conquered rather than a friend to be welcomed.

We were looking the other day at an old English print depicting the arrival of winter. Here was a cheerful procession winding its way through a sparkling woodland scene. There were gay heralds tootling along ahead, and capricious, frolicsome jesters cavorting alongside, and happy courtiers in the train, and in the center of it all, borne along on a festive throne, was a very jolly character. His cheeks were a nice mulled red, his eyes roguish and clever, and there was little doubt about what kind of evening he would order for himself as soon as he reached a stopping place. There would be sheltered warmth, and good food and drink, and relaxed companionship, and great wide jokes, some of them good because they were old and familiar.

Now this is exactly the kind of fellow winter really is, and those who refuse to let their corpuscles dance his tune have only themselves to blame.

Jottings from the Burrow

When we first came into this hole in a hillside, and pulled a comfortable blanket of leaves and grass in after us, we had small intention of retaining function of any kind. It would be enough to sleep. And in fact it is a long sleep from which we are now waking, a deep, refreshing, peaceful nullity in which we haven't had a care in the burrow. We are not exactly sure what time of year it is, but certain sounds from the highways as well as shifting radar from the zodiac lead to the guess that it must be approaching the new year.

If so, that means we have at least slept through the Christmas season, with its indigestion, strain of relatives, and aftermath of bankruptcy. Of course, if we had to, we would accept all these just to get that true feeling of Christmas spirit when it comes. But for once, this being the year of years when we are carrying out an old threat of hibernation, it is pleasant to be able to look back and imagine the spirit, without the strains.

As we muse here, in our comfortable darkness, we also find it pleasant to wonder what the weather has been. We have been having playful, half-conscious nightmares, in which we imagine ourselves unhibernated, and plunge ourselves into all kinds of unpleasant emergencies, always, however, waking up to find ourselves safe and comfortable, here in our burrow.

How relaxing to wake up and find that the furnace had not failed in the middle of a zero night, nor has any pipe frozen, nor has any car stalled!

Other might-have-beens occupy our time. Did we miss out on a white Christmas? Has there been an owl in the barn? We find such wonderings just as refreshing as knowledge, and then we dismiss them and go blank again.

That is the great peace of the burrow: its blankness. We curl here for days on end, suspended in animation and thought, lulled and comforted by an even body temperature, not very lively, after all, in our curiosity about what we may be missing in the outside surface world. Our thoughts are half-thoughts, and our questions demand little or no answer, and we feel no pain in problems that are not solved. We are in a wonderful hazy world of a contented drowsiness, and we set it down here, for the record, that this hibernation was nothing short of an inspiration.

And if it is, by any chance, the season of resolutions, we would set this down too: that we hereby resolve, whereas and whereas we have never had it better, to hold an open burrow, February 2, so that all our friends may come and envy us our hibernation.

But for the moment we can feel our drowsiness, the blessed drowsiness, returning, the sleep stealing through our veins, the thought recorder going dim, and we are, obviously, about to begin a new year unconscious. What a quaint ironic parallel between New Year's in and out of the burrow!

Progress Report

The sun has now come to the point where it sets nineteen minutes later in the afternoon than it did two weeks ago. From now on, the day will be lengthening itself steadily, at both ends.

We apologize for our persistence, year after year, in passing on this brand of intelligence. We feel a little shy about confessing that this turning point, this march toward fuller sun, becomes each year a little more precious, a little more important. It is all, we suppose, the result of the one-corpuscle type of existence. And because the one-corpuscle being yearns for spring and summer, even for the type of heat we had last August, it assumes that all other beings are equally impatient, equally ready to be cheered by any slight factual detail that illustrates the promise of the good seasons returning.

There is nothing like the stars of a winter night, appearing, suddenly, after the sky has been cleansed by a fall of snow. There is nothing like the sweetness of cold air, clean and pure. There is nothing like the deep inside stillness and comfort of an evening when snow is falling. There is nothing like the pinks and mauves and purples and variable grays and the steel blues of a winter sunset. And there is nothing like having, along with the enjoyment of these things, the knowledge that there is also coming the sweet scent of a June meadow, flecked with white and gold.

Zero Midnight

There are various things to be said about a cold spell, most of them reiteration of the fact that we don't like it.

Beyond that it has, however, like every other extreme in the weather, its stimulation for the sense and mind of man.

That is particularly so if it is a cold spell paced by a waxing moon. We do not know that midnight shadows on the snow are more impressively cast, or that the tracery of a giant tree against the sky is more detailed and delicate, or that the moon itself and its companion stars are any brighter or more glorious because the temperature happens to be at a certain level. If there is any real change involved, it is more likely to be located in the human eye, and in the sense perceptions behind it, these being sharpened because man, in zero weather, considers himself to be living in some dramatic emergency.

Whatever the cause, a zero midnight is surely the best of all times for looking at the winter world. And as the eye follows the alternation of dark and white, of shadows and traceries, in patterns leading away and over the hills, one hears things too: hidden bells tinkling where the brook is finally frozen over, the dull, muffled boom of the pond, straining to freeze-burst its banks, the faint, electric crackle of a star.

The Colors We Think We See

Ignorance does have its satisfactions.

For many years we have been noticing, whenever we step out into winter twilight, that winter is the best season for afterglow colors—that the reds and the greens of the frosty horizon are brilliant and rare. We have also thought we could notice a particular excellence of color in winter dawns.

Now comes science and goes into a lengthy, involved rigmarole to the effect that atoms of oxygen and sodium are somehow activated, in winter months, to provide the night sky with special colors.

This would be an acceptable display of knowledge—if science stopped there. But science goes on, to assert that lovely and brilliant as these winter colors may be, no one ever really sees them except scientists, because it takes special apparatus to view them.

So the winter sky possesses very lovely reds and greens, but we, poor ordinary mortals, can never see them. Until this scientific announcement interfered, we were journeying along, quite contentedly, under the illusion that we did see these colors any clear twilight or dawn. But when we go out, of twilights, now, scientific expertness joins us, and then it takes an act of faith to make us sure we really see anything. It is strange, how explanation of the beautiful sometimes insists on making it vanish, and sometimes almost succeeds.

Taming the Chuck

"If Candlemas is fair and clear, there be two winters in the year."

"Half your corn and half your hay you should have on Candlemas Day."

Groundhog Day maxims were usually worked in somewhere in the dispatches of the late Jennie H. Church of the town of Willington, one of the great country correspondents of yesteryear. But one year Jennie turned her attention from the maxims to the woodchuck himself and gave rather precise instructions for making a pet of one.

To make a proper pet, Jennie advised, you should get a woodchuck before his eyes are opened. Further, you should discard all specimens not born when the stars of domesticity and amiability were in the ascendant. You should be prepared then for a combination of affection and playfulness, the latter sometimes posing something of a problem.

In that case, said Jennie Church, you should realize that "it is better to rule by love than fear."

Ever since, on Candlemas Day, we have thought of corn and hay and cloud and sun and of the proper gentling of woodchucks and of Jennie Church, with some suspicion that her maxim was intended for more than chucks, and was her way of trying to shorten the winter in the minds of men.

Vertical Ease

Even when attacking a suet ball the downy woodpecker will, if possible, seek an absolutely vertical stance directly underneath the food, pecking up, even though there would seem to be much easier perches and angles for attack at the side or top.

To the human eye, this stance looks difficult. But like all uncorrupted children of nature, the downy is merely doing what comes naturally, and that is, of course, the easy thing.

If the downy sat alongside or on top of the suet ball, like any other bird, it would be abandoning the easeful pleasure of sitting on its own tail. The downy's tail is the closest evolution has come to duplicating one of those folding umbrella stick seats dear old ladies carry around with them at English garden parties. It is full of stiff spines, rather than mere feathers, and whenever the downy takes vertical stance its tail braces stiffly against tree or suet and provides a comfortable sitting position.

If the downy perched horizontally, this stiff spine of a tail would be merely a troublesome sail in the wind, promoting instability instead of anchorage.

What looks most difficult to us, then, is the easy, sensible thing for the downy woodpecker, especially when another of its special assets is noted. If the downy attacked the suet ball from anything but the vertical position, it would be throwing away that unique gift of nature which divides its toes into two front and two rear instead of the three front and only one rear in our usual feathered friend. That extra rear toe, along with the stiff fan of a tail, clinches the perch, and the case, for the downy. It knows exactly what it is doing, pecking up at its suet.

Salubrious Days

Is there any better tonic for living than a climate that ranges from 15 above at night to 35 above in the afternoon, that has an air both windless and dry, that has its sun rising through frost mist and its moon lavishing itself on a white world?

Days when every breath is a tonic, when the sun is a gradually waxing promise, nights still and clear boasting both

Jupiter and Venus in their sky, dawns when factory smoke rises straight up, twilights when the horizons are green and rose—what more dare one ask? Where could there possibly be a life more salubrious?

We are forced by pleased experience and reviving logic to concede that a perfect day in any one season is the equal of a perfect day in any other season. This, just as we had almost formed the rigid opinion that winter was one season we could possibly do without.

The Neat Brown Shape

Ever since we first made his acquaintance we have been captive to the pert, smart, uninhibited, almost too well adjusted winter cheer of the chickadee. Surely he is a dandy, the Beau Brummel of the snowdrifts, the Lord Chesterfield of the winter noon. He is friendly and unafraid. And he sings his cheerfulness at telling moments—in the storm at dawn, in the fading swirl of a sleeted twilight. Surely he is perfect in all ways, and now that we have become used to his friendly gallantry, we doubt that we could ever get through a winter without him.

The song sparrow's conquest of our heart has been a slower, less glamorous process.

In the being of the song sparrow there is that touch of modesty—or perhaps that artistic understatement of beauty—which always, in love affairs, wears well, and produces more endearment with the years. Never glamorous, but quietly beautiful, never striking, but delicately lovely, never overfriendly and demonstrative, but sharing life and season in a comradeship both constant and discreet—in such qualities the song sparrow has been winning our affectionate respect.

It is true that for much of winter the song sparrow has no

voice, so that it is only in our mind that the neat brown shape retains its sweet long trill.

But the other afternoon, in the sleet, when the black and white and gray had finally been soaked and battered into a loss of neatness and luster, the ordinarily less spectacular brown and white and spot and stripes grew more lustrous and bewitching, as the quieter, more enduring beauties always do in rain.

Snow at Night

Snow, like a good many strong, conquering things, can be silent. It does not feel compelled to announce its coming by a patter on the roof, or a beat against the window. It settles on the lingering oak leaves without so much as a rustle.

Noiseless itself, it brings quiet and hush to its hostland. It closes down on the brook and muffles its ripple and babble. It mutes, into an artistry they could never manage by themselves, the whistles and groans of the diesel trains in the valley.

It is a blessing upon the road. There is no traffic, except for the senseless periodic endeavor of the snowplows, which are doing their best to make it impossible for anyone to enjoy the privileges of declaring himself snowbound.

There is a time, then, on an evening in which snow is falling, when a road becomes good for walking again, when each flake of snow that falls against the face is a guarantee of privacy and security. On either side, the world stretches warm and white and clean, its houses silent and cloistered, its hushed meadows suddenly extended toward the night horizon as their fence lines disappear, and the road itself a direction devoid of urgency and seeming to lead, if anywhere, only to more peace and calm and quiet.

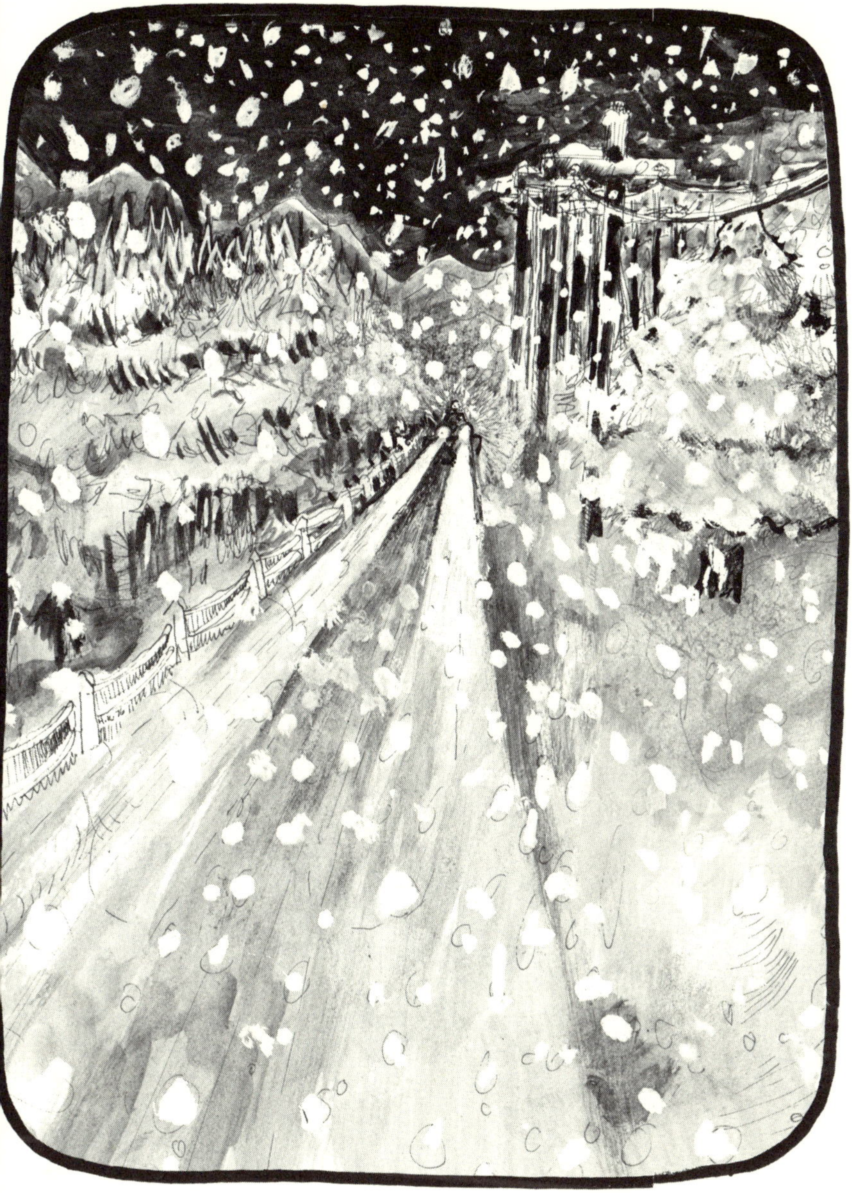

The Gentle Hussar

If there was ever a character who is the innocent victim of his own plumage, it is the blue jay. Because he looks bold, he is labeled bold, when he is really as timid as a wren. Because he looks dashing, he is considered a braggart, which he is not. Because other birds fly away when he flies close, he is considered a bully, when his real motivation is an endless quest for company and friendship. Whenever he tries to join people at breakfast, everybody suddenly leaves the table. When he would like to pass the time of day, everybody suddenly has an errand to do.

Now and then, in some sad and angry compliance with his own fate, he may try to play, for a moment, the role of the handsome braggart and bully.

But he has no heart for it, and soon relapses into a wistfully resigned acceptance of his world as it is, a world of being misunderstood, reviled, and ostracized.

Now surely our modern wisdom has taught us one is not responsible for the plumage one is born with, that a mock aggression really betrays the lonely, aggrieved heart. Surely the least society can do is to stop judging everything on the basis of that French hussar uniform, and give the jay its chance to become a well-adjusted bird.

A Drawing of Curtains

This winter's snow-encased weeks have been excellent for the restoration of that original country silence in which normally unnoticed sounds begin to be heard. There is a sharp single report, like that of a firearm, which comes out of the contraction of a great tree braced against zero weather. There is a reverberation like underground thunder from the expansion of a pond freezing out against its banks. A brook that is frozen over still gives an audible reading of the stones in its bed. The wind makes its least sound riffling through thin stands of dried weeds. There is a crunch of the snow underfoot that varies according to the temperature—shorter, sharper, and squeakier as the thermometer gets lower.

Linger alongside a bird-feeding station whose display of sunflower seeds has just been replenished, and the soft, rapid-fluttering whir of chickadee and titmouse wings will come in closer and closer, like a drawing of curtains on all sides.

Other Dividends at the Feeder

We feed the birds not so much to save the birds as to bring them closer. That is the whole proposition: the bird must come to *our* table placed where *we* decree if it wants to be saved from cruel winter famine. Conceivably, somewhere, the human being does exist who would be willing to place his or her bird food out in some invisible dispensary, with no guest book, no windows opening upon it, no way to watch arrivals and departures, and no entry at all, for the host, into the endless display of the foibles, virtues, cupidities, affections, graces, and even the occasional nonsense of the guests.

At feeder distance men and birds have a healthy way of getting along together without ever touching—touch, as one thinks of it, is the ultimate token by which we contrive to *own* people and things—that is seldom achieved in relationships with wives, husbands, children, cats, dogs, lovers, or even flowers.

But the ultimate overpowering reason for bribing birds to come closer—the experience that takes the human being back to the feeder again and again as if he or she could never be satiated—is that experience of color that can be provided only by the free and living bird at close range, within ten feet of the natural eye.

A cedar waxwing, gray and indistinguishable in the distance except for its crest, and often, in the reference book, unnaturally garish like color television, becomes an exotic jewel of tints never otherwise manufactured when he lights on a feeder just outside the watcher's window. Many of the colors that reveal themselves when birds can be brought that close are beyond our charts, our pigments, our words, and our senses.

The richest returns, at the feeder, often come from species least likely, seen from a distance or from the plates in a book, to be considered especially worthy of invitation. A drab mockingbird, noticed at first only because it has shifted its territory north in recent years, didn't establish a real welcome for itself until, at the feeder the other day, it turned its back, always gray in book or on garden post, and disclosed its real color. It was still gray, no doubt, but with a luminous filtering of brown, a blush of chlorophyll, and a suggestion of low-toned iridescents in a combination—once again words cannot report what the eye thinks it can see.

The most overwhelming sight that could ever come to a feeding station would be the female tanager, which Peterson describes as "dull green above and yellowish below, with brownish or blackish wings." Some of us have been close enough to the female tanager in the fields, on days when her husband was not commanding all our attention, to know that is woeful understatement.

A Thaw of Brooks

We negotiate the winter months in bondage, half of gratitude, half of fear, to elements we seldom see or touch. Veiled from us in some subterranean furnace mystery, choked within the cylinders of some motor, or slinking along inside the imitation skin of a blanket, there is that fire without which we might not live.

And in constant battle with this image of fire there is the concept of ice—usually, in our most routine awareness of it, some vast expanse girdling Hudson Bay and giving off great wind breaths that sweep down toward, around, or into us.

Between the elements of fire and ice we lead a winter existence in which every moment is in doubt; the fire may fail, the ice prevail.

Addicted to the thermometer, we are precariously indifferent to other standards for living. The fire stands off the ice; we run the season's gauntlet between them, one half of us always a little too warm, the other on the verge of being too cold. We come near the end of our passage without much feeling of any kind, a surly numbness with the world as we would never have made it.

When, at last, spring starts to emerge, we know it first by a restoration of respect for things about us, a rebirth of loyalty to life, a softening of our partisan judgments, an ending of our harsh loneliness.

With such harbinger instincts coursing through us, we are off, once more, for the life of the free and a long season's list of things we can see or touch: a redwing on a high elm, warm ground on the south side of an old house, a bluet, a lilac bud, a patch of sun in a courtyard, the thaw of brooks and faces.

Query

Who is this visitor, who deafens our midnight with Aristophanic choruses, who smiles at dawn and weeps at noon, who flatters us with disarming cheer at one moment and pelts us with the hail of a whimsical disregard a moment later?

Who is it opens the forsythia bush during one warm flow of southern air, and who loosens, at last, the long and unbelievably tight buds of the shad-blow? Who throws these delicate bluet nosegays down from the sky, careless and flustered as a bride? Who kneels, fragrant, to the fragrance of the arbutus?

Who floats with the meadowlark, and chortles with the robin, and peals with the plover, and still has music of her own?

Whose footsteps leave the meadows green, whose hair kites and curls among the clouds, whose hand touches so lightly and endearingly, whose sweet presence drives all but the cleanest thoughts away?

Who is the only one who never need yearn to be in England when all the world wants to be there? Whose name is itself a rippling, liquid poem?

Softer Now

All things grow soft. The ground beneath the foot, first soft, and then firmer for plowing and gardening. The bud, swelling and expanding for bloom out of its long tight winter curl. The song sparrow, middle range like an opera star singing for her own pleasure. And the heart of man, leaping out of the dour mold of winter to encircle his world and the people in it. The rain, no longer hard and crystalline as it falls. The sky, with the first clouds that are April, and no other month. And, in the fourth twilight of the month, soft piping from the pasture. And the stars, with Venus so ample and soft a true Puritan would drop his eyes.

Frolic

Spring comes to each species at a particular time and in a particular way. The other night it was the muskrats who suddenly were touched by the magic wand.

Their display began in low key. One young fellow broke to the surface of the pond, swerved casually around a wide arc, lay quiet and motionless in the center of the pond, and then swam slowly toward a clump of old grass on the shore.

There something—perhaps the first shoot of new green inside the old clump, perhaps the fact that the shallow shore water still retained some warmth from the late-afternoon sun—touched off the muskrat's love for his new season. He threw himself back from the shore, swam a short splashing circle, went back to shore, and pushed off swimming again, this time at such a pace that his body rose well out of the water like the hull of a speedboat while his feet were high enough to create splash with their movements—almost a walk, or run, on top of the water.

These exploits apparently sent sound-wave summonses to other muskrats still in their dens. Soon another muskrat broke the surface, and then another, and three more. If our readers have not already abandoned all faith in our accuracy and reliability as a reporter, this is what then went on:

Short- and long-distance speed trials.
Formation swimming.
Follow the leader, with quick scampers over shore areas.
Water polo, the favorite strategy being the head-on collision at highest swimming speed.

As we said, spring comes to each species at a particular time and in a particular way. We happened to be pondside on the night when, for our amphibious pond family, it was pure frolic.

A Nation of Gardeners

We are a nation of gardeners who in each cycle somehow forget how the earth will crumble between our fingers, and we come into each new growing season only half aware of what its performance is going to be like. We are not prepared for the way the daffodils and tulips stand up to the sun. The majesty of the panicled lilac is more than we expected. The infinite confusion of flower and winged samara and catkin and leaves of which our more familiar trees are capable overwhelms us and torments our most casual walk.

We have to be careful what branch we leave too long in an office vase, for fear it may send out roots and by touching some momentary sentiment in us seduce us into a foolish commitment. There is a perennial virginity in us that never quite prepares us for, but is always ready to surrender to, the fruit trees in blossom, the misty impressionism of a spring border, the geraniums and flags of Memorial Day, the spinsterhood of the petunias, or the moss rose in its jeweled sheath.

In our letters to our friends, it is this or that which is in bloom, or has just come to table from the garden. The evidence involving us is overwhelming. We are all, in whatever occupation or location, either on our way away from the land or on our way back toward it.

It is the land holds the reality and the reference; half in wonder, half in disbelief, we scratch around in it not too far away from or beyond that earliest man who poked a stick into it, and we always uncover some earlier root, or some forgotten flowering, or some still ungerminated seed which is of ourselves.

Our gardening of knee and mind provides some replacement for all those philosophies that so long ago lost themselves in their mutual labyrinthian negations, for those religions that no longer relate themselves to what human beings actually do or believe, for all those tonic therapies for nerve and blood once located inside the necessities of life. And it may contribute something to the eternal search for the human identity.

Who am I? Where am I? Why am I here? are all questions that can be answered successfully if one can say: I am the one who holds this cabbage seed and is about to implant it in this earth so that, having germinated, it shall wear its existence in some purpose and dignity.

Nothing but the land takes and bears so large a burden so well. Nothing presses back so reassuringly when we lean on it. It bears with equal buoyancy the feathery frond of fern and the many-celled office building and the light knee of the gardener and the heavy thought of man. We had forgotten, once again, how good it is.

Complaint

For the record, an authentic April shower is like this:

The birds are working happily in the sun, but some of the nesting materials are a little too dry for bending. A meadowlark whistles up a pretty pink cloud with a sprinkler system attached. The cloud turns the sprinkler on for half an hour and then heads toward the east, becoming a rainbow. The warm sun comes out and the birds stop singing and get to work again. Everything is just right, warm and moist, and germination is almost a visible ripple down garden rows. The sky is pure blue again, and there is no wind, just a movement of cherry blossom fragrance across the land.

That is the authentic April shower, the kind that brings flowers in May, or sooner. It is not a two-day continuous chill drizzle, which keeps man and bird alike from working, which rots seeds instead of sprouting them, and pelts all fragrance to the ground.

❧

Tree Toad Mating Day

The first swamp sound of spring is that of the peeper, which for the benefit (or confusion) of the uninitiated, we identify as *Hyla crucifer.*

The peeper is a night singer, and his shrill, clear pipings make a nightly chorus once the trend toward spring weather has become firmly established.

The second swamp sound of spring is that of the tree toad, another creature entirely, technically identified as *Hyla versicolor.*

The voice of the tree toad is huskier and more blurred than that of the peeper, and unlike the peepers, the tree toads form a true swamp chorus only on one or two spring days.

Today is, or at least began to be, while the rain was still warm, tree toad mating day. On such a milder than usual April morning, some spring-fevered member of the community hies himself down from his tree and to a patch of water and there he sets up a call.

This call he makes with the aid of an unbelievably expansive air sac in his throat, which bellies out, and then subsides gradually with a sweet whirring sound.

When this first call is made the whole community of tree toads begins moving with one mind and one purpose to the same patch of water. Then there is sex and song, all day long, until the landscape throbs with the throatings of hundreds of nature's children on nature's business. The peepers do the early courting. The tree toads take the new season to water bed.

Obituary for a Brook

We watched a bulldozer burying a brook the other day, and it was obvious from the nimble skill with which the operator slashed and slammed at his target that he felt himself to be wielding the right instrument in the right place, to be doing something that should have been done long ago.

The bulldozer was making foundation space, between two existing houses, for a third house, and thus bringing into use, long after the street in question was originally built up, a stretch of land previously devoted to the uneconomic purpose of sustaining a brook.

What the buriers of brooks have in mind is clear enough.

They are closing over an annoyance, an infection, a potential flood, a waste of valuable footage and frontage.

We have jotted down a short list of other things they are closing over. Our list includes alders, autumn leaves, books, bottles, bridges, calamus, cowslip, cress, dam, darning needle, flag, frog, gentian, gurgle, hellgrammite, lily, messages from Lorna Doone, minnow, mosquito, moss, muskrat, rapids, shiner, skates, snail, snake, stones, tinkle, treble, turtle, violet, willow. Other people, remembering some afternoon once spent face down over a pool, may wish to add something to the list.

Violets

To lift the violet out of the literary pages in which it has been pressed as a symbol of all things shy and modest, and then to examine it in its natural shape and beauty, is to discover that it is the most voluptuous of all wild flowers. Once we look at it clearly with our adult, experienced eyes we find its structure to be that of open, entrancing imitation of the physiology of sex, providing, of all flowering things, the most luxurious and convenient welcome to those storied bees from whom we all learn our first lessons about the mystery of life. And then it may be we, and not the violet, does the blushing.

To recover from such embarrassment, one goes back to an even earlier and more innocent relationship with the violet, in which farm children found that picking from a crowded bank was a delirium of spring delight. With violets, a bunch, or bouquet, was not subject to any artistic limits; there could be as many stems as a fist could hold—the bigger the bunch that could be tendered as offering of boy and spring to the lady of the home, the better. Certain things small boys think they wish they could do forever. Picking violets was one thing they often did for at least an afternoon of forever, with hands that were grubby and greedy and, in the final tendering act, beautiful.

The adult mind may toy with its idea that the violet provides an exquisite suggestion of sex, but what it really depends upon as warranty of generation succeeding generation is a new appearance of violets at the kitchen door—fistfuls.

Soil and Soul

All the officialdom that might remotely be connected with the question of whether the average American should plant a vegetable garden this year has divided itself into two camps, one of which busies itself urging Mr. American to have his garden, while the other concentrates on the prospective waste of seeds, small crops, poor hourly rate of earning, and generous backache.

Neither camp concerns itself with the true reason why every individual who has the slightest instinct to garden should do so. It's a question of soul and soil, the latter being the place where many a man discovers, for the first time in many years, that he is a possessor of the former.

The crop of vegetables may be uncertain, but the harvest guaranteed his inner life when a man begins to delve in mother earth is as certain and plentiful as the backache. And it, more than vegetables, more than physical exercise, is the real return that is always awaiting him when, in response to an urge as old as life upon earth, he finally turns back to the soil.

In the very first act of deciding to have a garden there is a profession of faith that in itself is cleansing and strengthening. He has, perhaps, lived decades in the rapid swim of an artificial civilization. But now he has at last come back to a willingness to work with sun and soil and water and take what they spin out.

So doing, he has begun to make his philosophical peace with the world.

From that point on, the return grows always richer, and the peace deepens. Not till he has run it through his fingers does he give the soil the filial affection it deserves. Every individual seed that pushes through is an eloquent sermon in human contentment, a supremely rational, yet miraculous, accomplishment which weaves itself into the core of his being. Even the ants, spoiling a row with their mass industry, point morals and truths that do not have to be formulated to be sensed.

A few square yards of garden soil can hold and expound all the secrets of the world and life. These personal discoveries become part of the existential strength in him. The earth is home to him at last, a source of knowledge, and the mother of all philosophy, not just a useful gravitational aid that makes it possible for him to stand on it. Never doubt it, a garden does wonders for the soul.

May Evening

The robins sang past dark. Sirius, the last vanishing trace of winter sky, kissed the western hill and said goodbye for another year. The apple blossom gleamed white in the twilight, but still held its fragrance close. On some evening soon, a degree or two more mild, with an earlier fall of dew, it will loose this fragrance, diluted enough so men can breath it, on the gentle shifts of night air. A duck whirred between earth and the moon.

Earlier, the sun of late afternoon had brushed the green lawns into velvet, and highlighted the yellow-green of the birches on the hill, and played hide-and-seek with itself among the young leaves of the elms, and warmed the field so that work in it was like some clear, tranquil dream of another world, another world free of the complication and misery sometimes found in the style of living men alone, among all creatures, select for themselves.

And, on the perfect May evening, it *is* another world, so clean, so fresh, so beautiful, so mild, so full of thoughts as innocent as lambs, and loves upon which there is no shadow, that the only human instinct is to have it last forever.

Then, a bit fiercely, one turns to the spring world again, knowing that it is not forever, and that all one can do is drink deeply and store it up, and use it, a memory at a time, against the press of other moments and other moods. If ever one moment could justify all of life, it would be such an evening in May.

The Fraternity

Through all the temperate zone the greatest fraternity the world has ever known is preparing for its annual rites of similarity and brotherhood. On New England hillsides and on black-earthed western plains, in the cloistered fields of England and between the hedgerows of France, in the broad and monotonous regularity of the rectangular fields of Germany, over the collective farms of Russia, and the rice fields of China, to the terraced volcanic soil of Japan, the members of the human race who live next to the soil are all in unison.

Powerful or weak, varied in race and color, they are all fundamentally alike when it comes to their membership in the great fraternity of the seed. Wherever a seed is placed in earth, there men are sharing the same feelings and thinking the same thoughts, making the same overture to mother earth, venturing the same kind of effort, and nourishing the same hopes. They are so completely like each other at this moment of putting the seed to earth that one wonders how any kind of basic difference between them in any other matters could be imagined to exist.

Distractions

The crab apple had become, overnight, a solid mass of white bloom. The summer-sweet, thanks to a tint on its open petals, and thanks to some buds still unopened, was delicately pink.

Between the summer-sweet and the great ash—on which, this morning, for the first time this spring, a touch of green appeared—a young elm, of some thirty or forty years, presented a small-leaved shimmer against the sky. The sky, just rain-washed, had a streak of pink cloud running through its blue. The pink streak seemed to run into the apple bloom and lose itself there.

The air was busy with flight and song. No bird could stay silent or stationary.

A little later on, when the sun began to steam off the raindrops just fallen, all the scents lying dormant in this scene would begin to mount the air. There would be a meeting, in the sun patch on the grass, of the light perfume from the apple and the deeper fragrance from the first opening of the purple lilac, by the house, and the white lilac, by the brook.

A little later, if the sun kept shining, the finches would flock suddenly to the lawn, and lose themselves among the massed dandelions, until the dandelions themselves seemed alive and capable of short flights.

Later on, the pair of orioles, still in the careless phases of courtship while they are waiting for their own familiar elm to festoon and hide their nest site, would come swooping into the apple bloom. Orioles flashing into an apple tree in blossom are like one of those rare moments in music or literature when there is suddenly created the surprise loveliness that is beyond description, beyond all anticipation on the part of the artist, beyond all reaction except a quick awed stilling of the heart.

We knew all this was about to happen, if we waited. We were a little late getting to work this morning.

Russets Bloom Last

Apple bloom is like life in that, by the time we think we may be able to sit down and enjoy the beauty of it, we notice a petal is falling.

The bloom is only one brief perfect phase in the cycle that leads on to fruit, and to seed, and to the leaf falling, and then to sprouting and budding again. It is the whole cycle we ought to treasure, with its special sadness and its compensating hope and its broader promise that if this is the way it is with the apple, it may be so with other productions of nature, including people.

Still, in petal-falling moments, it is human instinct to wish for and to reach for any kind of prolongation, even for a day, of the blossom phase. And it is here that the russet plays its part and proves worth planting.

The fact that the russet blooms late is a surprise dividend; not, of course, the reason it was planted. Russets are planted, nowadays, because of obstinate memories of apple barrels down in cool, earthy cellars, and of the sweet taste russets held, years ago, when they got to the wrinkly stage. It is at least partly pursuit of an illusion, like all efforts to recapture childhood flavors. By the time the tree is bearing, one discovers that it is the idea of having russets, rather than the actual eating of them, which is more pleasant.

But then one also discovers that the russet has at least one charm for adults that childhood never even noticed. The day the other apple trees begin losing their petals on the May air, the russet petals begin to open. If one is late for the perfect moment, one moves to another part of the orchard.

The Straightest Line

The swamp this spring has a low water level and has dried out more than ducks like for breeding, hatching, and rearing a new family. Changing the happy concealment of bogs and grasses for the relatively public life of nesting near the shore of an open pond has involved some degree of adjustment for one mallard we know, and for the rest of the wildlife complex normally centered on the mallard's pond and swamp.

Since the mallard is required by his role to sail almost constant patrol off that point on the shore where his mate sits hidden on their nest, he has been forced to become a tame mallard, disciplined to endure the human eye and, even more tensely, the human footfall approaching along the shore. During one of the first early mornings of his performance, the neighborhood crows discovered that he had taken over the particular spot on the shore where they gathered for their morning drink, and some curious tableaux ensued, with the green-headed, maroon-prowed mallard standing inside a circle of blackcoats. There was even one afternoon when the red-winged blackbirds seemed to be swirling overhead in some vague attack plan, as if they found a mallard in the open more disturbing than a mallard half concealed.

The next time we looked, however, the pond-and-swamp area seemed to have settled into a peaceful routine, with the mallard patrolling like Nelson's flagship after victory, the crows patronizing a new pool created by a happenchance log dam across the brook, the blackbirds down on their willows, the swamp itself as dry and inhospitable as the mallard and his mate had known it would be. The whole vernal season, it seemed, was waiting for the moment when the mallard would lead forth, from a still hidden site along the shore, a flotilla of six or seven or eight ducklings strung out in the straightest line known to navigation.

Drop and Dodge

A spell of weather like this—hot, humid, with a fusion-prone warm moisture even in the nights—provides a demonstration of power not even man's fateful experimentation with the atom has equaled.

You have to be careful, in such weather, how you handle seeds. To be entirely safe, you step back as you drop them. It is a sensible precaution to have a hoe in one hand as you drop the seed with the other, so the burst can receive some cultivation while it is still young. If the seed is scheduled to produce a plant subject to beetles, aphids, or blight, it is best to have some dust or spray handy too.

It is in such weather that cutworms, fastening themselves to a tender stalk for their preliminary bite, suddenly find themselves dangling helplessly in upper foliage at a great height, and wonder why the fire department doesn't come.

It was in such weather that Jack dropped a seed and saw his beanstalk rising out of sight.

Once, in such weather, there was a man who thought it would be nice to have a circle of sunflowers in the center of his garden. He made the mistake of standing inside the circle as he dropped the seeds. He spent a lovely, lonely summer.

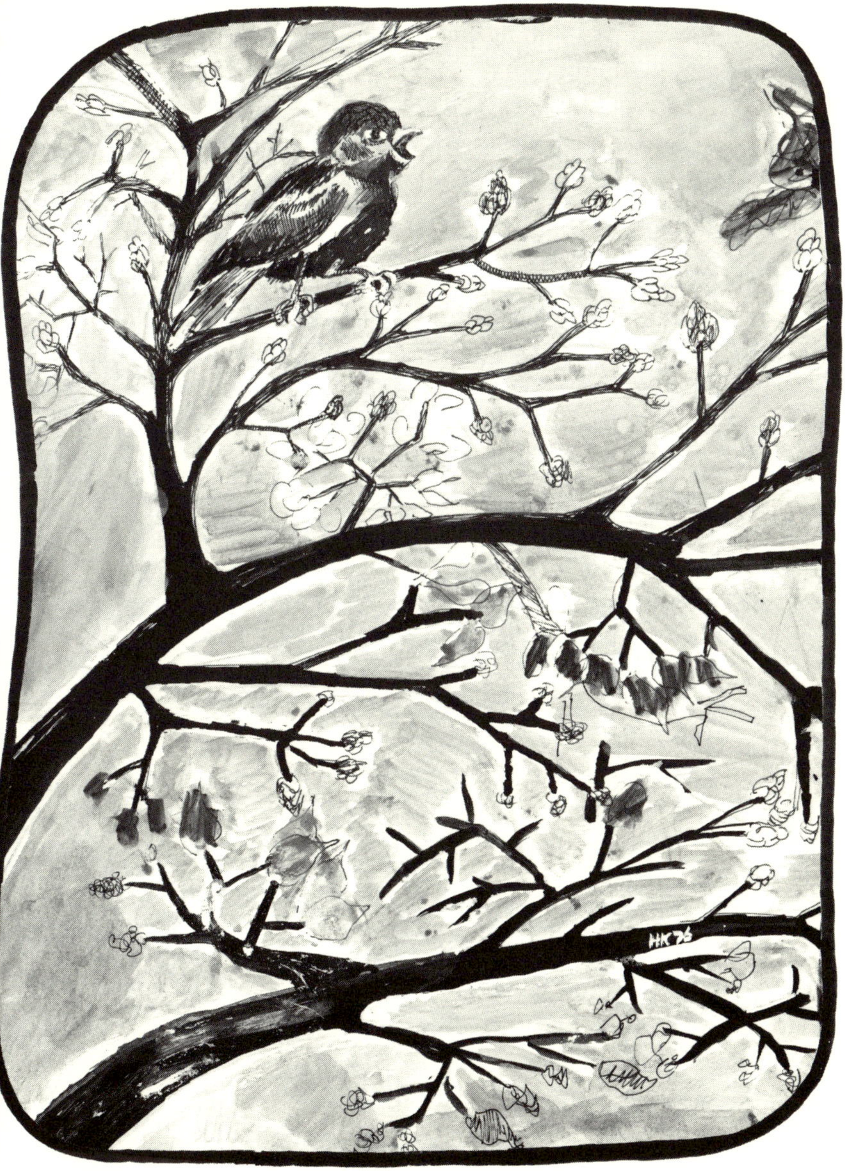

Choices

This is the time of year when, beset by swiftly paced abundance, we must pick and choose among our loves. There's to be an end of May, of lovely May, almost before we draw breath, and yet any one of many sights and sounds is worth a whole month's enjoyment.

It would be a thrifty thing to spend at least a day watching the orioles as they flit and flash and whistle and call in all the scintillating courtship that is going to end with a basket cradle on the underhanging tip of the elm.

Another day might well be spent looking at the white lilacs with sunlight and cloud shadows moving across them.

May has the perfect sun. We could take a week just turning under its friendly touch.

There is a corner in the wood where the dancing wood nymphs tripped and left lady-slippers behind them.

At the top of the hill, corn is breaking ground for a summer chapel.

There is a brook where wild geraniums nod.

Clover rises sweet and green.

Dirt is lovely to look at, and stand in, and take in the hands.

The landscape is soft, as if it were winding along some French river.

May rain is glad rain.

We can resist none of these, and possess none.

Loves Among Plants

First with us, year after year, is corn in all its stages, drilling its way up through the soil, forming, immediately, the graceful chalice it will hold for rain and dew, pushing up its tassel to send sex and pollen down to the silks that lead into the fruitfulness of the ear, and finally producing the one taste that, more than any other, proclaims that summer has come to the dinner table. The poetry, the science, the sensuality, and the historic mystery of corn (it has never been found growing without the assistance of man, leading to legend that some kind god placed it in the hand of man) all combine into a lifelong love affair for us.

The culture and growth of Bibb lettuce is by comparison uncomplicated and unspectacular. One lines out a long garden row, and groups a half-dozen seeds every six or seven inches in the row, covers them lightly, waits, if the warmth and moisture are just right, three or four days for germination, and then, as soon as the seedlings are tall enough to grasp between thumb and forefinger, thins each group down to one single plant. A delicate application of side fertilizer, close but not too close, and a decent amount of attention from the hoe, plus three or four weeks time, will produce a squat, modest-appearing shape, perhaps seven inches in diameter, that is ready for the beheading knife.

It is immediately thereafter, as it reaches the vegetable sink, that the particular lettuce one Jack Bibb developed out in Kentucky a century and a quarter ago reveals its miracle. It now contains more leaves than anyone ever saw developing. Each is of a perfect structure and proportion, as if it had been constructed to be a sea shell for a Botticelli Venus to be born from. The endless layers of leaves come off clean and spotless, with no trace of dust blown in or spattered in by rain. There is no stray invasion or trace of insects. No other product of the garden comes so close to being fit for spotless linen and china without kitchen processing of any kind. It can be encountered in the restaurants of San Francisco at something like a dollar a leaf. The ordinary gardener can be profligate with such perfect art, with only the expenditure of a few cents for seed, and no more bend of back than any less distinguished vegetable requires. The taste may be something less than that of oak leaf, which, with lucky management, can be teased into a similarly tight-curled shell formation, and different from the more charactered tang of the variety named salad bowl, but it is forever crisp and tender. Anyone who grows sweet corn and Bibb lettuce knows what gardening happiness really is.

Spring Riot

We have just spent a day within earshot of a read-in by a brown thrasher. The unbridled, irresponsible mimicry of this cocoa-colored bird is not distinguished by very much art. His imitations are instantly recognizable, and instantly regrettable; if he were doing poets, one could be horrified by the torrent of bad Yeats, bad Hopkins, bad Thomas. What the brown thrasher does do is birds, all of his fellow birds, including poets and nonpoets, and everything he does seems good to him. The other day he was doing blackbirds and robins and song sparrows and towhees in rash echo of authentic songs all around him, but he was also drawing on his memory of other years for ovenbirds and thrushes, who had not yet arrived on his scene.

Invariably, the imitation was so easily identifiable that one knew immediately that it was supposed to be, say, an oriole, and yet so joyously off-note that one also knew it could never have been produced by an oriole.

Such is the biology, the entelechy, of the thrasher that he finds a few afternoons of spring riot quite enough to set his whole world back on an even keel. All the rest of the year he leaves the reading-in to his somewhat more professional cousins the gray-trousered catbird and the mockingbird, and is himself a modest brown bird, casual on the lawns.

Occlusive Singer

We were fortunate, the other day, to catch the thrasher in the full old-time tide of his mimicry, for he no longer indulges himself and us as freely as in pre-mockingbird days.

Within the last half-dozen years the mockingbird, moving north into New England and multiplying, has progressed from the status of welcome stranger and curiosity to that of nuisance. Bird people who first found the invasion from the Southland a romantic affair are beginning to group the mockingbird, in their emotions, with such long-established nonfavorites as the starling and the blue jay.

The main trouble is that once a mockingbird establishes itself in a territory, with its full repertoire of imitations, the amount of time left open for legitimate songbirds to make themselves heard is limited. Even the other species of mockers bow to the competition. The thrasher may seek new territory. The catbird sits mute. Unlike the thrasher and the catbird, the first of which used to join riotously, the second modestly, in the song of other birds, celebrating their talents with some affection, the mockingbird sings occlusively.

For their first few years in the North, the mockingbirds

seemed to have left behind their habit of singing at night. But last year they began occasional night sessions, and this year they have developed regular midnight-to-dawn routines in imitation of the killdeer, the meadowlark, the cardinal, and the oriole.

The mimic is shutting the authentic music-makers out of their own songs, if not by monopolizing their singing time, then by giving their songs back to them so crudely that they become discouraged from producing the pure thing.

Cloistered

The bloom fades, more swiftly than it came, and we watch May turn from a flower into a landscape. The dandelions go, and let the lawn appear. The blossoms blow from the trees, and the new leaves mass together against the sky. They, in turn, have their perfect week or two, before the caterpillars move out of their webs, before the blight comes to the silver on the birch. The violets, a visible blue carpet two weeks ago, now nestle and hide deep in meadow grass. The alfalfa furls and curls toward that perfection which demands the knife of the mower. Even the ash, at last, has cast its flowers and shapes its massive dream of summer peace. The elm laces the foliage of privacy about the oriole's nest.

The landscape closes its open spaces, the geometry of winter is blotted out, the fields wear green fences, the woods grow impenetrable and wild, the eye shortens its focus, and the heart lengthens and slows its beat. This is as close to cloistered innocence and peace as earth can come.

Like an Ode

Of the poets we have under our thumb at the moment, only Wordsworth, not always the most lightsome fellow in the world, comes close to writing as if he owned the month of May.

Housman turned the month into a climax of thundershowers beating on tavern windows; Shakespeare somehow associated the mood of May with that of his villains, when they were "full of spirit" or when their crimes were "broad blown, as flush as May"; not even the Elizabethans did as much for May as their reputation and our imagination give them credit for; one could assume that perhaps such poets, being of the British climate, found May a heavier month than ours.

But then Wordsworth gives us May, forever and wherever, exactly as we all, in either hemisphere, recognize it, and so proves that it is not the forwardness of the climate, but the vein of the poet, that is decisive.

It was on a "sweet May morning" that Wordsworth chose to have his "Intimations of Immortality." "Land and sea," he wrote, "Give themselves up to jollity,/And with the heart of May/Doth every beast keep holiday."

And in the end Wordsworth promised to join in the festival, which he exhorted to continue: "Then sing, ye birds, sing a joyous song!/And let the young lambs bound/As to the tabor's sound!/We in thought will join your throng,/Ye that pipe and ye that play,/Ye that through your hearts today/Feel the gladness of the May!"

This morning of Wordsworth's choice was, in clinical detail, the only kind of morning light enough and clear enough and pure enough and translucent enough to offer the proper scientific conditions for the commuting between worlds and consciousnesses and existences Wordsworth wished to undertake. This was the morning he had to wait for, if his intimations were ever to lift themselves off the ground, disengage themselves from the gravitational pull, explore their universe freely, and still find clear, cool passage back to landing and report in the poet's mind.

Such mixture of scientific and poetic viability still makes the May morning. One is flung free; barriers dissolve; thoughts are cosmic birds; existence grows weightless and love has more megatons than anything, and if one knew how to feed such data into the machine, one could produce a computation that would stand, like an ode.

※

Big Maple Year

Late into May, when even the slow ashes and oaks had turned themselves green, the maples of this Eastern countryside were still massing beiges, saffrons, and pinks more reminiscent of very early spring or the first turn of foliage in fall than of the usual May fullness.

The colors came from a heavy yield of samara, the winged seeds, so thickly clustered on the maples this year that they took both space and vigor from the normal foliage process of the parent tree. When, by the end of the month, the colors had finally fallen, they left the maples sparsely and thinly leaved, with lots of sky to fill before they could offer anything like their normal midsummer density of shade.

Meanwhile, the flight patterns of the samara, with the double seeds grown together on the same stem and two flying wings that soar and glide and spin with a freedom and versatility that not even a bird can equal, have been exhibiting, once again, something in nature that our aerodynamicists have never been able to simulate in their wind tunnels.

It is, as one watches them scurrying up and past in a May wind, the nearest thing there is to absolutely free flight—an example of how man might cavort in the air if he were really liberated. It is also, obviously, such a high and extensive use of the principles of free flight and fall that it has to result in the placing of maple seeds in every conceivable location for a chance of germination and growth—a multiplication of chances as profligate as that which, on some yet undated occasion in the past, first brought the components of bacterial life together somewhere on the planet.

Thanks to this efficiency, there will be, about twenty years from now, a very large class of young maples in our swamps and on our hillsides, and if any foresters of the time are still counting rings and making statistics, they will reach the conclusion that this must have been, for some reason, a big maple year.

※

The Making of Summer

One swallow does not make it, but scores of them have been taking their flying dips in our evening pond.

One reading of the thermometer does not make it, but it is surprising how quickly a second day of that reading can bring the full tide of warm ease into that winter-pinched corpuscle.

One bath of warmth doesn't now, as it will later, add inches a day to the corn, but you would be surprised and thrilled if you could see what feverish energy it releases underground.

One field turned golden with buttercups, one deep-set nest with its full quota of eggs, one trout shattering the mirrored stars, one unheralded attack of noonday torpor—none of these makes a summer fully guaranteed against an instant return of cooler weather.

So it is not summer. But there is no valid reason for inflicting such legalism upon your senses. Let these run with the green-banked brook, swell with the seed, dream in the sun.

Again and Again

Our reason, and sometimes our jaded senses, may try to mislead us into thinking our business here is pointless, empty, futile.

Yet that verdict on life is one that threatens us only at passing moments. In spite of it, although the press of circumstance may be dull and seemingly relentless, there are imperishable true things we live by. Without them, life itself does seem nothing but slow death. But with them even death has its portion of fitness, its beauty.

They constitute the why and the purpose of living. They are the reason we keep on. They are the reward for keeping on.

We grope and grub our way along, strangers and children in a world darker than it used to be. And then, on the various planes of our individual lives, something of a momentary miracle occurs. Some bewitching sign of moving seasons distracts us from the ordinary and directs us into a higher plane of sense and feeling. Something we first notice almost casually underfoot stimulates us to see, clearly and warmly, the vistas of existence located out beyond our own circumstance. Some leafy reminder of the cycled conspiracy of earth and sun reestablishes the good connection between ourselves and others and between all of us and that earth and sun. We may happen, in a sudden, unexpected pause, to hear the silence that is the sound of the infinite. We may feel a sanctified part of something beyond ourselves, something we can possess although we can never quite touch it.

Once it happens to us, whatever the experience and whatever our level, we are never the same. Through all the web of our days, there is a shining thread. It leads on and on, always reappearing. By it, we are born again and again, like summer.

❦